petitcollage

LORENA SIMINOVICH

petitcollage

25 EASY CRAFT AND DÉCOR PROJECTS FOR A PLAYFUL HOME

POTTER
CRAFT

NEW YORK

Published in the United States by Potter Craft, an imprint of
the Crown Publishing Group, a division of Random House LLC,
a Penguin Random House Company, New York.

www.crownpublishing.com
www.pottercraft.com

POTTER CRAFT and colophon is a registered trademark of Random House LLC.

Library of Congress Cataloging-in-Publication Data
Siminovich, Lorena.
  Petit Collage : 25 easy handmade projects for a playful home / by Lorena
Siminovich. — First edition.
     pages cm
(print edition : alk. paper)
  1. Handicraft for children. 2. Children's paraphernalia.
3. House furnishings. I. Title.
  TT157.S528185 2014
  745.5—dc23
                    2013022415

ISBN: 978-0-385-34508-8
eBook ISBN: 978-0-385-34509-5

Printed in China
Design by Sara Gillingham Studio
Photography by Thayer Allyson Gowdy
Illustrations by Nora Aoyagi
Cover design by Sara Gillingham Studio
Cover photograph by Thayer Allyson Gowdy

10 9 8 7 6 5 4 3 2 1
First Edition

THANKS...

To my parents, Barbara and Daniel, for nourishing my creative side from a young age

To my design community in San Francisco for inspiring, sharing, and existing!

To my husband, Esteban, for his loving patience and unconditional support

To my editors, Betty Wong and Camaren Subhiyah, who guided me through my first craft book

To my daughter, Matilda, for being my muse and always-ready model

To my agent, Adriana Dominguez, for pushing me into good things

To my design team, Annie Tsou and Nora Aoyagi, who helped make Petit Collage, with a special thanks to Nora, who made this book possible

To my dear friend Sara Gillingham for designing this beauty of a book

contents

foreword

by Holly Becker, interiors author and stylist, founder/editor of decor8blog.com

As a stylist, interiors author, and design blogger, my life is a nonstop creative adventure that leaves me feeling deeply nourished and blessed. It seems in creative disciplines there is a constant flow of never-ending inspiration to drink from; yet no matter how many new products I'm exposed to or talented makers I meet, I never tire of the beauty that exists in the world. Whether this beauty enters my life first, or I had to dig for it, I immediately know what is fresh and unusual and can spot a mile away the gem that stands out from the pack or the artist with that special something. For me, one such artist has long been Lorena Siminovich and the work that she produces through Petit Collage, her company in San Francisco, and now this gorgeous book that you're holding in which she so lovingly produced under the same name as her fun-loving brand.

I remember discovering Lorena's work online in 2006 when she launched Petit Collage and how inspired I was by her cohesive collection, overall vision, and creative talent. Her sweet patterns and motifs, with obvious mid-century flair, spoke to me as I felt little ones and the young-at-heart would be captivated by them. She has that certain something. I also recall the day in 2007 when I learned that Anthropologie commissioned her work to be sold in their stores nationwide and I wrote about it on my blog, decor8. I felt so proud; we both began our companies in the same year (2006) and her rising popularity and success inspired me to keep working hard, too. Since then, Lorena has grown her brand by leaps and bounds to include everything from flash cards to books, prints, and puzzles—all in her whimsical colorful style that is so very *Lorena*. When we had the chance to meet years later at Anthropologie for my own book signing, I immediately felt she was a kindred soul who had traveled a similar journey as I and we'd both stayed on course and followed our dreams—two women with a passion for making things beautiful and for bringing a little more joy into the world through our work.

Petit Collage is clearly a labor of love crafted with curious eyes and little hands in mind (with the help of big hands, too!), evident with each lovely flip of the page. In fact, the many photographs and carefully considered projects inspired me to break open my craft cabinet and get to work. After poring over each page, I've concluded that it's the perfect book for mothers-to-be like me and also for children, parents, aunts, uncles, and even grandparents who want to sit down and craft together with their grandchildren.

With a baby due to arrive, I've decided to give the Bunny Wall Clock project a try along with the owl door tag for the nursery, which I am currently in the process of decorating. This book made me stop and think that I should use my hands more before running out to purchase everything for my baby because the handmade projects will always be the most special. My mother and aunt made so many things in my nursery when I entered the world and long after, which had a direct impact on my own creativity and how I viewed the world around me along with the profession that I ultimately chose for myself. I was reminded through Lorena's book to continue the tradition in my own little family—to create special things by hand.

I love the whimsical combinations of colors and materials used throughout mixed with her contemporary graphics and practical application and easy approach. For instance, the window film cutouts are just perfect for adding a graphic touch to a space while concealing a not-so-perfect window view and the friends coat rack is the perfect mix of practical and creative.

One thing that came to mind as I read *Petit Collage* is that we must never allow crafting to become a lost art, despite how we live in an age when everything is being outsourced and digitalized. Crafting with our children is not only helpful for their own self-discovery and self-esteem, but also shows them what goes into making things, which builds a greater appreciation for the possessions we're surrounded by that we often take for granted. Crafting together also forms a bond between adult and child and gives both a chance to explore and play.

Like Lorena, I believe in "surrounding children with beautiful, well-designed art work, and handmade accessories." This approachable, heartwarming craft book will allow you to do the same, helping you draw nearer to your little ones, bring more joy into their lives, and add a spirit of happiness to your home through objects you've made and infused with your own unique personalities. Isn't that what family life should be about?

Petit Collage is for families large and small who want to make, bond, show love, enjoy simple pleasures together, and build lasting memories through the art of crafting by hand. I hope that you enjoy it as much as I do. Now, back to making my bunny clock . . .

Happy crafting!
xo
Holly Becker

introduction

My childhood was a colorful collage in which different elements came together to make me the designer I am today.

I was born and raised in Buenos Aires, Argentina into a family of European immigrants from diverse backgrounds. When I trace my influences, the images that appear in rapid succession—almost like looking out the car window on our long summer drives—are the European mid-century objects in my home, museum visits with my graphic designer dad, and the lush Latin American colors that surrounded me. I was fortunate that my early interest in art was encouraged by my family. For as long as I can remember I took painting and drawing classes, and then sculpture and printmaking. My earliest memories of art making include the joy and pride I felt creating something unique and personal by hand. These memories also include the struggles when my ceramics broke in a kiln or when my mom didn't know where to store my latest "masterpieces," but that didn't dim my love for making.

Years later, my love of art transformed into a passion for graphic design.

I was working as a creative director for a gift company when my husband was presented with a wonderful opportunity and we moved from New York to San Francisco. Little did I know what the future would hold, but, as they say, things happen for a reason! I was telecommuting with my company's New York office, spending endless hours behind a computer, and although I loved my job, I was longing for those days when I made things with my hands. One night, only minutes before meeting a pregnant friend, I decided to attack my secret stash of found and vintage papers and make her a collage of an owl family. All I had were scissors and glue, lovely papers, and a repurposed vintage card as the canvas—nothing fancy. But I remember the excitement of the cutting and pasting, my heart beating a little faster in anticipation for the results, and then the happiness looking at the final piece. And just like that I was crafting again!

A few weeks later, hooked by the intoxicating feeling of the handmade process, I created a mini-collection of collages on wood plaques and took them to a few stores. They placed orders and my company, Petit Collage, was born. Fast forward a few years and items from our line of collage-inspired decor and playthings are found in homes around the globe. We have expanded from wall decor to mobiles, dolls, toys, and gifts— all inspired by paper, modern patterns, and natural materials such as wood and bamboo.

Shortly after starting my company I discovered yet another of life's greatest joys: motherhood. Seeing my own child grow and my friends' families flourish made me realize how much life changes with kids, and how important the space where we live is. The home we make reflects and extends who we are as a family and what we surround our children with—from furnishings to accessories, toys to textures—can help influence and fuel their own creativity. So this book is about several passions of mine, which I hope you share: meaningful handmade objects, well-designed goods, vintage and upcycled materials, and colorful and bold living for modern families.

On the pages that follow, you will find easy as well as slightly more elaborate projects. There are a few where you can even enlist kids to help. Most of the projects require very little new purchasing and are suited to reusing what you already have or can easily find. And since I'm a person who needs quick results, you will find several project ideas that offer a fast turnaround. If you are reading this at night, yes, you can still make it to that baby shower in the morning with a lovely handmade gift.

All of the projects can be personalized or customized, whether this means adding a name or an initial, or matching a room's color scheme or a child's favorite hue. I encourage you to keep an open mind about the materials you might use, take your own approach to these projects, and make them personal and relevant to your family. I'm more excited about you adding your own unique spin on these ideas, rather than following every step of these projects exactly the way I made them.

Now is the time to find that old map you were saving for who knows what, the tickets to that concert you've been holding on to, the giftwrap from your daughter's first birthday, and even that small table in the closet that is missing a leg. Now is the time to visit flea markets, garage sales, and to discover old things that are now ready to be transformed into some pretty cool new things. Happy crafting!

FINDING INSPIRATION

You can find inspiration in everything
(and if you can't, look again).*

▶ Much of this book is about reusing, repurposing, and recycling materials. It is also about "re-looking" (yes, I made that up).

▶ Look at the pattern inside an envelope or on a piece of wallpaper and use it for fantastic (free!) new material.

▶ Pick colors from a beloved painting, or a favorite piece of fabric.

▶ Think about the feeling you get from a color, then pair it with a neutral, now think about it again.

▶ Design a whole room around one random object that catches your eye.

▶ Recently my daughter fell in love with a fluorescent pink and red koinobori, those Japanese fish-shaped wind socks. She wanted to hang it in her room, so I seized the opportunity. Soon enough the colors of that fish became the color palette for her whole room. Of course I could have chosen a palette I saw at a kids store, or in a decor magazine, but the fact that we built a room around a meaningful object made the results a lot more personal.

▶ Give yourself permission and the confidence to take your design instinct or your inspiration out of context and execute it in a new way. I found typefaces and fonts for my next catalog in a restaurant menu, inspiration for an art print in vintage toy packaging, and pattern inspiration in a tray discovered in a summer house.

▶ Many times we push ourselves to go somewhere or look at something to get inspired. While I'm a big endorser of flea market trips, museum outings, and book browsing, the reality is inspiration comes from a state of mind and not a destination.

▶ Inspiration comes to you wherever you are, and if you are present, she will find you. Now it is up to you to choose what you do with it!

*The title of a wonderful book by fashion designer Paul Smith, which has become my design motto.

how to use this book

Everything you wanted to know before using this book.

ARE THE PROJECTS EASY?

Absolutely! Most of the projects are super easy and have a great ratio of little effort to big reward. Follow the level labels on each project to determine which is right for your skills and time frame.

◻ EASY Projects that can be made in 1 to 2 hours with widely available materials.

◻ INTERMEDIATE Projects that, although simple to make, may require multiple steps, extra drying time, or a special tool or material.

◻ ADVANCED Projects that require either wood cutting, drying overnight, or many steps to accomplish.

ARE THE MATERIALS EASY TO FIND? WHAT ABOUT THE PRICE?

Unless you are a minimalist, chances are you will already have a lot of the materials in your house. If not, most materials are easy to find at garage and estate sales, flea markets, or any paper, art supply, or craft store. Since you can create many of these projects by repurposing materials, the cost can be little or next to nothing. A few of the larger projects require a trip to the home improvement store for lumber. Please refer to Resources for information on sourcing wood.

DO I NEED LOTS OF TOOLS?

You will mainly need scissors and a craft knife. Some projects also might require a drill.

WHAT ABOUT THE TEMPLATES?

The templates are in the back of the book and are very easy to follow. Unless otherwise noted, they should be reproduced at 100 percent by photocopying, scanning, and printing. That said, many of the templates are interchangeable and you can resize them easily to suit your own needs.

CAN I CHANGE THE DESIGNS OR COLORS?

Yes and yes! Please do! The main idea for this book is that you can customize and personalize most projects with your own colors, textures, and names. Even something as simple as mixing and matching the papers you use will result in a piece that is unique.

One big tip: If possible, keep it flat! Store your papers in flat files or drawers. If you must keep them rolled, make sure you flatten them out a day or so before starting your project. It will make things so much easier and you will be happy you did.

CAN KIDS DO THESE PROJECTS?

The projects in this book are intended to be created by grown-ups, but that doesn't mean the little ones can't join the crafting fun! In a few projects I added a "Kid Fun" box with ideas for how kids can help you craft that don't require any extra materials than the ones already used in this book.

materials, tools, and tricks of the trade

I have to confess, as a creative and enthusiastic person, there have been times that having the right materials or tools has not been a priority for me. I've gotten so excited when inspiration strikes that I just gather whatever I can, and work in my own, sometimes chaotic, haphazard system. If I'm determined to make something, a wonky pair of scissors is not going to get in my way, right? Well, after ruining some more expensive materials and ending up with less-than-neat results, I have learned, as hard as it may sound, that being organized and having everything in its place can actually help my creativity.

And I've learned I enjoy the gathering process, making sure that I have all the papers and decorative items I want to use before the project gets going. After all, I check that all the ingredients are available before making a chocolate cake, so why would crafting be any different?

Following are the materials, tools, and supplies you might want to keep on hand to make the projects in this book.

vintage or recycled papers

Many of the projects in this book encourage you to use old or found papers or envelopes that you probably already have lying around your house. This may be my favorite topic in the whole book—finding great new uses for old materials—but I will contain myself and simply say: Keep your eyes peeled! Flea markets, garage sales, and thrift stores are wonderful places to discover interesting vintage sheets, but paper is everywhere. Check the mail, reuse cereal boxes, upcycle scrap papers and mementos. These beauties are waiting for you to give them a second life. Here are some favorites. I hope this ignites a eureka moment that has you running to find that forgotten box of old ephemera.

OLD MAPS

PAGES FROM DISCARDED BOOKS OR MAGAZINE ADS

VINTAGE WALLPAPER, FULL SHEETS OR SAMPLERS

RECYCLED GIFT-WRAPPING PAPER

MUSIC SHEETS OR SEWING PATTERNS

23

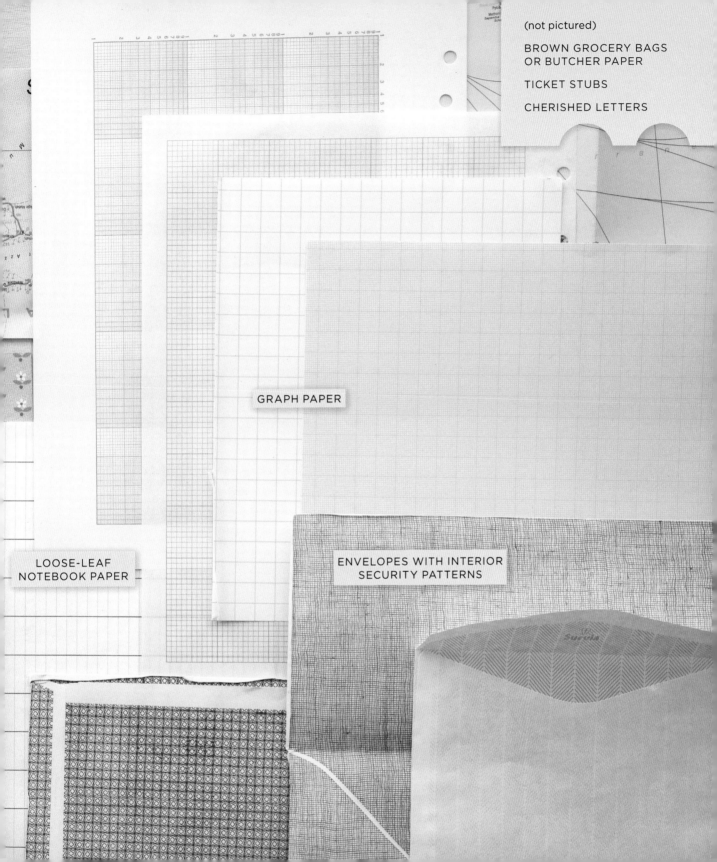

(not pictured)

BROWN GROCERY BAGS
OR BUTCHER PAPER

TICKET STUBS

CHERISHED LETTERS

GRAPH PAPER

LOOSE-LEAF
NOTEBOOK PAPER

ENVELOPES WITH INTERIOR
SECURITY PATTERNS

new papers

As much as I suggest recycling and reusing paper you already have, the reality is that some projects require a strong color or a large piece, so you will find yourself buying new paper. The best choices include scrapbooking and gift-wrapping paper, art store charcoal and pastel paper, and cardstock. Keep in mind a lot of the projects in this book require decoupage glue, so thin or handmade papers won't work. Avoid thin rice or tissue paper, as the colors can bleed and they can wrinkle. Also avoid construction paper, as the colors can fade. And as lovely as some of them are, heavily textured paper can be hard to layer and stick. Here are some papers that will work very well for the projects in this book.

HEAVYWEIGHT ART PAPER

GIFT-WRAPPING PAPER

SCRAPBOOK PAPER

ORIGAMI PAPER

19

make your own patterned papers

Some simple techniques can give you one-of-a-kind papers. Here are some ideas to try to make existing papers extra special.

PAINTING: To obtain an interesting printed sheet, paint over old book pages with diluted acrylic paint so you can still see the text.

PHOTOCOPYING: You can photocopy a beloved textile (think: vintage scarf or first onesie) to create some nice, ready-to-use patterned paper. Please note the copy should be made with laser printing and not inkjet home printers, as inkjet ink may bleed when wet.

STAMPING: Stamps are a great way to create patterns. Many household items, such as bubble wrap or erasers, make easy stamps; just use an ink pad and press. The green sample is made with little pieces of a rubber band pasted on a piece of foam board. The red sample is made with artist tape pasted with spacing on a found block of wood. The dots were created with the eraser at the end of a pencil.

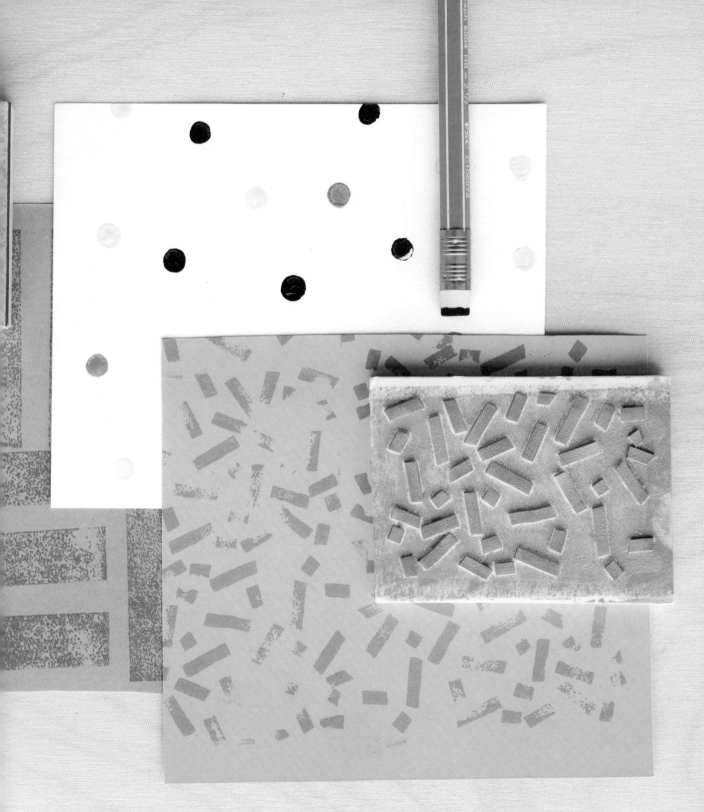

tapes and adhesives

Here is a brief guide to the magical things that keep it all together. You will find references to these glues and tapes in many of the projects. Some are specific to one particular project, so check before you stock up.

OFFICE SUPPLY
STICKERS

DECORATIVE WASHI TAPES

MULTIPURPOSE
SPRAY ADHESIVE

REPOSITIONABLE
MOUNTING SPRAY

ALL-PURPOSE
WHITE GLUE

MOD PODGE /
DECOUPAGE GLUE

PLAID®

CS11302

MOD

Scotch

Scotch

supe

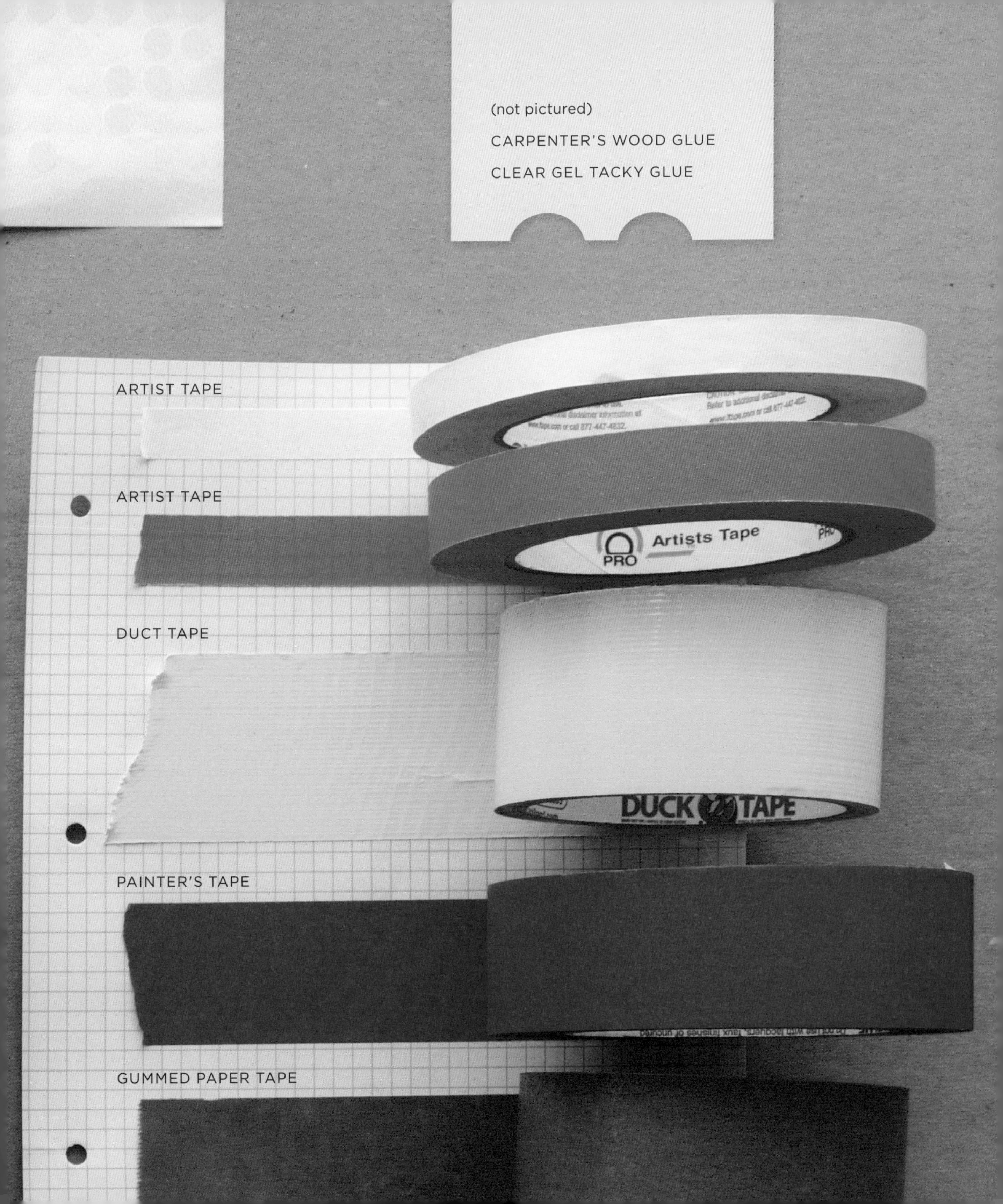

(not pictured)
CARPENTER'S WOOD GLUE
CLEAR GEL TACKY GLUE
ARTIST TAPE
ARTIST TAPE
PRO
Artists Tape
DUCT TAPE
DUCK TAPE
PAINTER'S TAPE
GUMMED PAPER TAPE

basic tools

My trustworthy tools of the trade. These make the job easier. The must-haves to create the projects in the book are a good pair of scissors, a craft knife, a pencil, and a ruler. Others are required on a project-by-project basis.

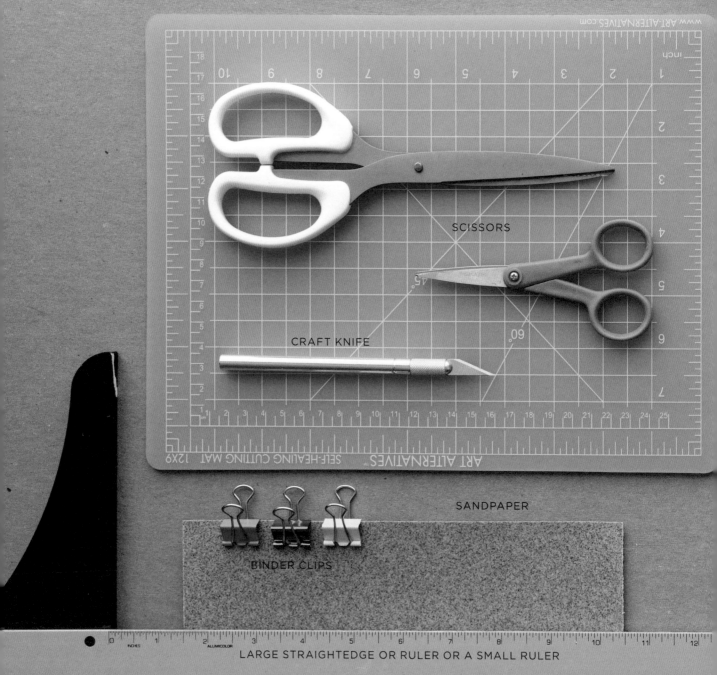

CUTTING MAT

SCISSORS

CRAFT KNIFE

SANDPAPER

BINDER CLIPS

LARGE STRAIGHTEDGE OR RULER OR A SMALL RULER

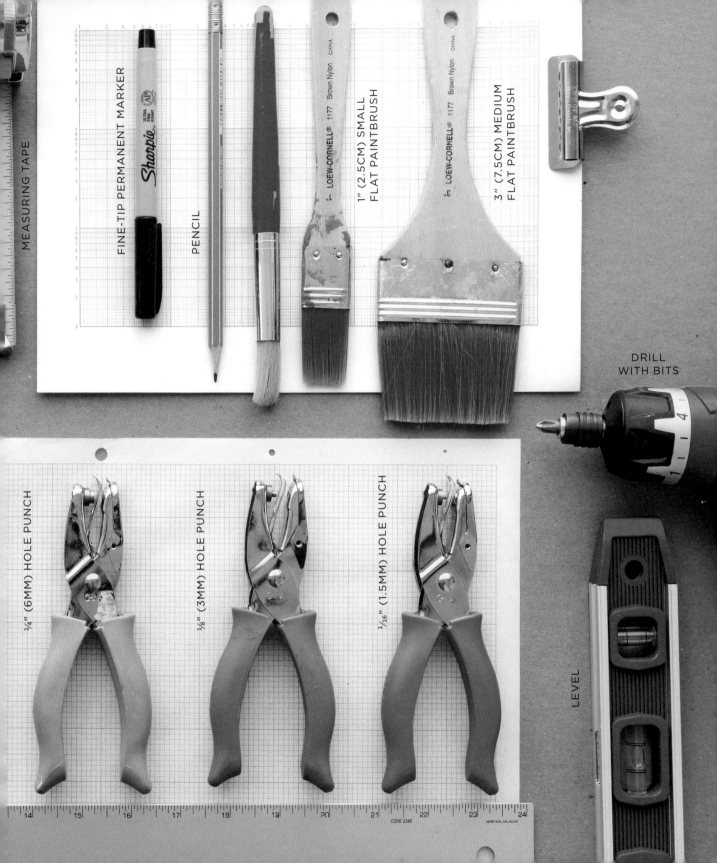

MEASURING TAPE

FINE-TIP PERMANENT MARKER

PENCIL

1" (2.5CM) SMALL
FLAT PAINTBRUSH

3" (7.5CM) MEDIUM
FLAT PAINTBRUSH

DRILL
WITH BITS

¼" (6MM) HOLE PUNCH

⅛" (3MM) HOLE PUNCH

¹⁄₁₆" (1.5MM) HOLE PUNCH

LEVEL

14   15   16   17   18   19   20   21   22   23   24

CODE 2280   MADE IN EL SALVADOR

1

ROOM TO GROW

I believe in surrounding children with beautiful, well-designed artwork, and handmade accessories. Kids spend a great deal of time in their rooms, as does the rest of the family, which is why these decorative projects have everyone in mind. This chapter includes a collage on wood that was the start of the Petit Collage line, as well as a mobile, which is a signature piece in our collection. Both of these are easy gifts to create and give. Other favorites include a toy bin that makes picking up toys a snap, and a bunny clock that will be used for years, first telling the time for naps and then later for school.

The beauty of kids and their spaces is that they grow, change, and evolve. As soon as you are relaxing because the nursery is done and looks great, you'll be replacing the crib in favor of more toddler-appropriate decor, making space for a play table, and not too long after, designing a headboard for a twin bed. It goes by fast, so keep this book handy and the crafting going.

JUST HANGING paper mobile

LEVEL: ▢ **FINISHED MEASUREMENTS:** 9" X 4½" X 4½"
(23CM X 11CM X 11CM)

MATERIALS

▶ Paper Mobile templates (page 130)

▶ heavyweight colored paper, such as construction paper or card stock

▶ decorative paper, such as assorted envelopes with patterned security interiors

▶ double-sided tape

▶ fishing line or monofilament thread

▶ screw-in ceiling hook or mobile hanger

TOOLS

▶ scissors

▶ binder clips (optional)

▶ ⅛" (3mm) hole punch (optional)

▶ pen

I have a special connection to mobiles. They are a big part of my Petit Collage line, and are my go-to gifts for baby showers. Mobiles provide such entertainment to the youngest children. Whether hanging in the corner of a room, or above a baby's crib, the spinning birdies will cause endless fascination. The instructions are for making a single bird, but once you get the hang of things, it is hard not to make more.

instructions

1. Using the templates, cut out 1 bird body and 1 flower stem from the heavyweight paper.

2. Cut 4 flower blossoms and 2 bird wings out of the decorative paper. I use binder clips to hold the template to the paper for easy precision when I cut.

3 Punch out the thread holes on the paper pieces where indicated.

4 Fold each of the decorative circles in half with the pattern side of the paper inside the fold.

5 Once each of the circle pieces is folded, use double-sided tape to adhere one half of the back of a circle to half of the back of another circle, making sure the thread holes align. Repeat with the remaining two circle pieces.

6 Once the halves of your flower are assembled, tape the flower stem piece

flat against the back of one of the flower halves. Tape the second two flower halves together to make a four-sided flower blossom.

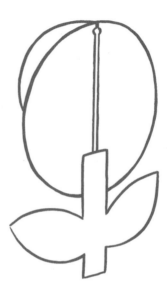

7 Tape a wing to each side of the bird body. Draw or make a small hole for the eyes.

8 Use a small piece of fishing line to thread the bird to the flower. Make a loop and tie the two pieces together securely.

9 Use a longer piece of fishing line to hang your completed mobile. Thread

the line through the top hole of the bird body, making sure you leave extra string if your ceiling is high.

10. Use a ceiling hook to hang.

11. Repeat steps 1–7 to create more mobiles.

12. Hang and enjoy!

▶ KID FUN

BIRD ORNAMENTS

Using the same bird template, cut one or several birds out of card-stock. Use a hole punch to make a colorful assortment of confetti, punching patterned or colored papers. Set up a craft station with the cardstock bird shapes, confetti, and glue, and let the decorating begin! For extra color, provide kids with non-toxic paint, office stick-ers, or whatever sparks your little one's imagination.

Try the tip in this section to make the birds more holiday or season appropriate using different color changes.

tips

▶ Color embroidery or sewing thread can be used as an alternative to the fishing line.

▶ Customize this birdie for a special holiday by changing the color palette. Make a Christmas cardinal hanging from baker's twine, or an Easter chickadee with a subdued pastel palette. Kids of any age will enjoy this simple gift.

ALEXANDER

HELLO WORLD

personalized
baby plaque

LEVEL: **FINISHED MEASUREMENTS:** 8″ X 8″ X ½″
(20.5CM X 20.5CM X 13MM)

A similar paper collage on wood was my
company's first product. It's a fantastic
gift. Make this original piece of art as
unique as your favorite wee one. It will
become a beloved heirloom and a bright
spot in a baby's room.

instructions

1. Using the templates, cut out 1 elephant,
1 elephant ear, and 3 drops from any papers you
choose. I use binder clips to clip the template
to the decorative paper for easy precision when
I cut.

2. Using the letter templates, cut out the child's
name from any papers you choose.

3. Brush an even coat of decoupage glue on the
wood plaque and apply the elephant pieces.
Smooth the paper with your fingers, if necessary.
Set aside to dry.

MATERIALS

▶ **Personalized Baby Plaque templates (page 131)**

▶ **Letters templates (page 128)**

▶ **assorted colored and patterned papers**

▶ **8″ x 8″ x ½″ (20.5cm x 20.5cm x 13mm) wood plaque**

▶ **decoupage glue, such as Mod Podge**

▶ **artist tape**

▶ **hanging hardware (optional)**

TOOLS

▶ **scissors**

▶ **binder clips (optional)**

▶ **1″–3″ (2.5cm–7.5cm) flat paintbrush**

4. Make sure the piece is dry. Apply a strip of artist tape horizontally on the wood plaque to establish a baseline for the letters. Apply another even coat of decoupage glue onto the wood plaque above the tape and apply the letters. Remove tape and set aside to dry.

5. Apply a final coat of decoupage glue to the entire plaque to finish.

6. Store-bought wood plaques are ready to hang from a screw in the wall. If you upcycled a piece of found wood to create this project I suggest purchasing hanging hardware in your local store.

7. Give as a gift or hang on the wall and make a mom happy!

▶ KID FUN

NAME PLAQUE
Using a second wood board or a fun canvas such as a paper plate, make an extra copy of the alphabet template so kids can cut out the letters of their names and decorate the boards to their heart's desire. This can be a fun door plaque for their rooms.

tips

▶ Save security envelopes from your bills. These often have great patterns inside.

▶ If bubbles appear under the paper as you are gluing it to the plaque, use a pushpin to make a tiny hole to release the air and smooth the area with your fingers.

KNOCK, KNOCK baby door tag

MATERIALS

- ▶ Baby Door Tag templates (page 132)
- ▶ two identical 4"- (10cm-) diameter cork coasters
- ▶ blue, yellow, white, and assorted colored papers
- ▶ assorted found papers
- ▶ decoupage glue, such as Mod Podge
- ▶ Clear Gel tacky glue
- ▶ 30" (76cm) length of ¼"- (6mm-) thick flat cotton ribbon or flat white shoelace

TOOLS

- ▶ pencil
- ▶ scissors
- ▶ black or brown fine-tip permanent marker
- ▶ measuring tape

LEVEL: ⬚   **FINISHED MEASUREMENTS:** 4" X 4" X ¼" (10CM X 10CM X 6MM)

New parents can be easily distinguished from others by their almost chronic shushing voice, fueled by the fear of waking up their offspring. I'm not judging, I was one of them. I have also received "the look" when being loud while somebody else's baby was napping. Let this sleepy or awake owl door tag alert others when quiet is needed.

instructions

1. Using a pencil, trace the circumference of one of your coasters onto the blue and yellow papers you would like to use as the background pieces. Cut them out.

2. Using the templates, cut out 1 owl head, 1 owl body, and 1 owl wing night from various blue papers for the "asleep" side. Repeat with various orange and red papers for the "awake" side,

using the owl wing day template instead. Cut out 4 owl eyes from white paper, and 2 owl beaks from yellow paper.

6 Draw in the eyes with a permanent marker on both owls, using the photographs as a visual reference.

3 Coat one side of each coaster with decoupage glue and apply the background pieces. Place a weight on top of each coaster and allow to dry completely.

4 Working one owl at a time, assemble and glue the "awake" owl pieces onto a coaster. Repeat with the "asleep" owl pieces. Allow to dry completely.

5 Coat the backs of the coasters with tacky glue and press them together. Allow to dry completely.

7 Cut a 30" (76cm) length of ribbon. Run a line of tacky glue around the edge of the coasters. Starting just below the owls' heads, wrap the ribbon around this edge. When the entire edge is covered in ribbon, adhere the end of the remaining length of ribbon to a point opposite the ribbon start point.

8 Now you know when it is *shhhh* time!

UP AND AWAY

bird growth chart

LEVEL: **FINISHED MEASUREMENTS:** 54" X 12"
(137CM X 30.5CM)

Look how big I am! Measuring a little one and marking their growth is such a childhood rite of passage. Growth charts are staples in the Petit Collage collection, so I created this one to be made of vintage papers and easily adhered to the wall. Let these birds witness your child getting taller and taller!

MATERIALS

▶ **Bird Growth Chart template (page 133)**

▶ **assorted patterned papers**

▶ **double-sided repositionable adhesive sheets**

▶ **artist tape**

▶ **adhesive numbers**

TOOLS

▶ **scissors**

▶ **pencil**

▶ **¼" (6mm) hole punch**

▶ **measuring tape**

▶ **level**

instructions

1. Enlarge the nesting bird template 200 percent. Gather papers you like and set them out in the desired order. Make sure that each piece of paper is large enough to comfortably accommodate the template. Since you will be flipping the template for half of the birds, you will want a lot of wiggle room.

2. Cut the repositionable adhesive sheets to fit the pieces of paper. Peel off the backing on one side

of your adhesive sheets and affix it to the back side of each of the chosen papers.

3. Cut out 5 left-facing birds using the template. Flip the template to cut out 5 birds that face toward the right. Use the ¼" (6mm) hole punch for the eyes.

4. Before permanently adhering the birds to the wall, I highly recommended that you first position the bird pieces as desired using loops of artist tape to quickly mount them to the wall. This is an important step, as they will be difficult to reposition once the adhesive backing is removed.

5. To place the birds, measure 14" (35.5cm) from the floor and mark with artist tape. This will be the bottom point for the first bird. Start with the bottommost bird first and work your way up.

6. To make sure the birds stack vertically, create a guide with a long vertical line of artist tape a few inches to the right of the bottom marker. Use the level if necessary.

7. Start stacking the birds using tape loops on the back. Make sure the beaks of the right-facing birds line up with the vertical tape guide.

8. Once the birds look good and line up nicely, one by one, remove the tape loop from each and peel off the adhesive backing to firmly adhere them to the wall. Remove tape guides.

9. To apply the measurements: Measure 16" (40.5cm) up from the floor and make a small mark in pencil in the center of the growth chart. Using a measuring tape, make small pencil marks every 2 inches (5cm) until you reach the uppermost bird. Adhere the numbered stickers directly over the pencil marks. Make sure you start your measurements with 16" (40.5cm) and not zero!

10. Ta-da! Let the flock do its job!

▶ You can create your own stickers with the child's age to use as milestone measuring dates. Take a white circle sticker and write "Today I'm 1," "Today I'm 2," and so forth, then stick it on the relevant height measurement on that given date. You can also create out-of-the-box milestones such as "Today I ate my first ice cream" or "First day of pre-school."

▶ If this is a gift, you can put all the adhesive-backed birdies in an envelope, and make a little note with hanging instructions, or you can make a coupon with "free application included." If you do the latter, you may as well throw in a "free babysitting" coupon too in order to make a parent over-the-moon happy.

▶ KID FUN

DECORATE WITH DECALS

You can use these decals to decorate furniture, label dresser drawers, or adhere to blank cards to give as gifts. Have your kids participate as a fun afternoon craft activity.

MY NAME IS . . . patterned letters

MATERIALS

- ▶ **found or purchased wood, metal, or cardboard letters**
- ▶ **assorted colored and patterned papers**
- ▶ **decoupage glue, such as Mod Podge**

TOOLS

- ▶ **photocopier or scanner**
- ▶ **pencil**
- ▶ **scissors or craft knife**
- ▶ **cutting mat**
- ▶ **1"–3" (2.5cm–7.5cm) flat paintbrush**

LEVEL: **FINISHED MEASUREMENTS:** VARIES BY LENGTH OF NAME AND SIZE OF LETTERS USED

A baby's name is such a magical thing to me. We often name them before we even know them, although their name will identify them for their entire lives. As they grow children take such pride and ownership of their names (it is often one of the first words they learn to write), making this project great for any age group.

instructions

1. Spell out a child's name using found or purchased letters. Create a paper template of the letters by placing the letters facedown on a photocopier or scanner. Draw a vertical or horizontal line through some or all of your photocopied letters. Cut out the shapes and the additional drawn lines.

2. Select the papers that you want to use to decorate each letter. Be mindful of colors and

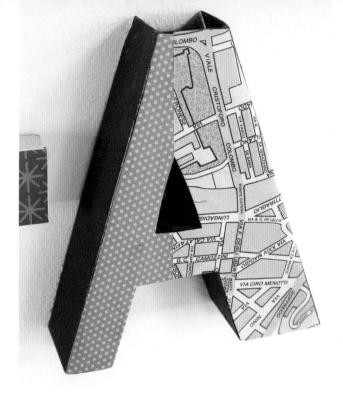

5 Once the edges are lined up, use the brush to add another coat of decoupage glue to the top of the paper, firmly adhering the paper to the letter. Allow to dry.

6 Hang letters from screws in the wall. If using vintage letters, buy hanging hardware in a local store.

7 Say their name, say their name!

patterns. You can experiment mixing and matching papers in each letter to create a patchwork effect.

3 Using the templates you created, cut out the letters from the decorative paper using scissors or a craft knife. Lay the cut paper pieces on the found or purchased letters to ensure there are no overhanging edges. Trim any excess.

4 To adhere the paper to the faces of the letters, brush each letter evenly with decoupage glue and then gently lay the corresponding paper cutout on top.

tips

▶ You can find vintage letters in flea markets or wood and cardboard letters in craft stores.

▶ Choose colors to match the room or simply use the child's favorite color.

▶ Play with the scale of the letters. A miss-matched arrangement with different fonts and sizes works best.

▶ Use papers with meaning, such as a map of a birthplace or photocopy of a beloved textile, for an extra special touch.

LEAN ON ME

cityscape wood veneer headboard

LEVEL: ⬜ **FINISHED MEASUREMENTS:** 34" X 36" (86CM X 91CM) (TO FIT A TWIN BED)

MATERIALS

▶ **Cityscape Headboard templates (pages 134–35)**

▶ **self-adhesive wood veneer**

▶ **artist tape**

▶ **various decorative washi tapes**

▶ **assorted round and star stickers (optional)**

TOOLS

▶ **utility knife**

▶ **large ruler**

▶ **measuring tape**

▶ **pencil**

▶ **level**

Story time, snuggles, and tucking in; bedtime is a big part of a kid's day and the bed is the centerpiece in their room. Sleeping under the city skyline is a child's dream come true!

instructions

1. Using a utility knife, cut out pieces of wood veneer to make the cityscape buildings: one 12" x 6" (30.5cm x 15cm) piece, one 16" x 6" (40.5cm x 15cm) piece, two 20" x 6" (51cm x 15cm) pieces, and two 24" x 6" (61cm x 15cm) pieces. See guide in template page. If possible follow the wood grain for easier cut.

2. Using the templates enlarged at 200 percent cut out the remaining pieces of the cityscape.

3. With the bed in place, mark the width with artist tape on the wall. Also mark the height of the mattress. Move the bed away from the wall. The cityscape when finished will measure 36" (91cm)

across. Measure this width on your wall, using your first tape marks to guide where you want the cityscape to be. Mark this length with fresh pieces of artist tape. To determine the base of where your cityscape will start, measure approximately 2" (5cm) below where the mattress hits the wall. Mark this with artist tape.

4 To apply the cityscape pieces to the wall, I highly recommended that you first position the pieces as desired using loops of artist tape to temporarily and quickly mount them to the wall. They will be permanent once affixed.

5 Use a level to ensure that they are perfectly straight. Make any changes as necessary.

6 Once ready, remove the backing from the veneer pieces one by one, and firmly adhere each piece to the wall, smoothing it down with the palm of your hand. Remove all tape guides.

7 Now that the cityscape is laid out, you can apply the details. For the windows and signs you can use washi tape. For the lights and other windows I used circle dots from office supply stores.

tips

▶ Build your own world and customize this landscape to the city of your choice! Broadway lights or Space Needle, you can be the architect.

▶ I used washi tape, artist tape, and office stickers, but any tape or stickers you have on hand will do. Be creative!

▶ This design is made for a twin bed but can be extended by adding additional wood veneer pieces for more buildings.

MOVE ON BACK!

wheeled toy bin

LEVEL: **FINISHED MEASUREMENTS:** LETTERS IN PLACE MEASURE APPROXIMATELY 4½" (23CM)

MATERIALS

- Wheeled Toy Bin templates (page 136)
- found wooden crate or bin
- decoupage glue
- artist tape
- 24" (61cm) length of ⅜"- (9mm-) thick cotton rope, cut in two equal pieces
- four 2" x 3" (5cm x 7.5cm) blocks of plywood (make sure the base of your casters is smaller than the plywood blocks)
- carpenter's wood glue
- four 2" (7.5cm) casters
- sixteen screws
- assorted colored and patterned papers
- assorted leftover or found papers

TOOLS

- sandpaper
- 1"–3" (2.5cm–7.5cm) flat paintbrush
- pencil
- drill with bits
- scissors

One of my (many) parenting frustrations is my underdeveloped Mary Poppins power for cleanup. Enter the rolling toy bin! Put together this beauty in no time at all, and make cleanup even faster. You're welcome!

instructions

1. Gently sand away any rough edges on the crate or bin.

2. Coat the exterior with decoupage glue using a wide brush. Allow to dry.

3. On the side panels of the crate, mark 2" (5cm) from the top edge of crate. Center a 4" (10cm) piece of artist tape under this line to mark where the rope handle will go.

4. Drill two ¼" (6cm) holes in each end of the paper tape for the rope to thread through, then repeat on the other side. Remove paper tape.

5 Thread 12" (30.5cm) rope through both holes, tying a knot at each end in the interior side of crate. Repeat on the other side.

6 Attaching the casters: Flip the crate upside down. Place a plywood block at each corner of the crate just far enough in from the edges of the crate so that they do not hang out over the "walls" of the crate. Trace the outlines of the blocks with a pencil and remove them. Most crates have a very thin bottom. The plywood blocks will be glued inside the crate for the screw to go through.

7 Flip the crate right side up. Using carpenter's wood glue, glue the wood blocks to the bottom of the interior of the crate at each corner. Allow to dry.

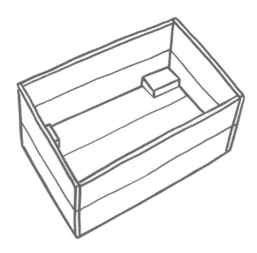

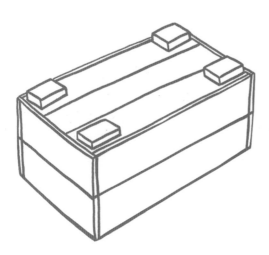

8 Flip the crate upside down again. Working one at a time, position the casters within the pencil outline of the plywood blocks and mark the mounting holes. Drill the holes and attach the casters using the screws.

9. Using the toy bin text template enlarged 200 percent, cut out the letters from the decorative papers. Apply the paper letters to the crate. Use artist tape as a guide.

10. Apply a final protective coat of decoupage glue and allow to dry.

11. Cleanup time!

tips

▶ Be choosy about your crates, they need to be clean and free of nails or splinters. You could do this project with old drawers, too.

▶ If you make multiples of these (yes, it can be addictive), you can number them for a nice graphic effect.

▶ If your crate has handles, skip the rope.

ABOUT TIME

bunny wall clock

LEVEL: ○   **FINISHED MEASUREMENTS:** 13" X 9"
(33CM X 23CM)

MATERIALS

▶ **Wall Clock templates (page 137)**

▶ **8" (20.5cm) wood embroidery hoop**

▶ **thin wood veneer**

▶ **clock mechanism**

▶ **corrugated cardboard**

▶ **assorted colored, patterned, or found papers**

▶ **felt**

▶ **Clear Gel tacky glue**

▶ **decoupage glue**

▶ **artist tape**

▶ **strong glue**

TOOLS

▶ **pencil**

▶ **scissors**

▶ **craft knife**

▶ **¼" (6mm) hole punch**

▶ **stapler**

▶ **cutting mat**

▶ **medium 3" (7.5cm) flat paintbrush**

▶ **ruler**

Find an embroidery hoop, add some wood veneer and throw in a few felt details. Presto! A bunny is born. Now add the clock mechanism and bring him to happy tick-tock life! Proceed to convince the kiddos it is bedtime. Bunny says so.

instructions

1. Begin by tightening the embroidery hoop to ensure that the hoop pieces are firmly locked together. Lay the hoop on the wood veneer, and trace around the exterior edge of the hoop with a fine pencil. Cut the veneer following the pencil line using scissors or a craft knife.

2. Mark an X at the center of the veneer with your pencil to indicate where to make a hole for the nose. The size of the hole will depend on the size of your clock kit. Use the nut of the clock kit to trace the diameter of the spindle of the clock kit onto the veneer.

3 Cut out the hole for the clock mechanism using a craft knife.

4 Lay the hoop on the cardboard, and trace around the interior edge of the embroidery hoop with a fine pencil. This piece will sit inside the hoop behind the clock face, providing support for the thin veneer.

5 Cut the cardboard just inside your traced line using a craft knife.

6 Cut a roughly ½" x ½" (13cm x 13cm) square hole in the center of the cardboard, using the veneer as a guide to find the center of the cardboard.

7 Using a ¼" (6mm) hole punch, punch out two eyes from any paper you choose.

8 Using the templates, cut out the 2 rabbit cheeks, 1 rabbit nose, and 2 bow tie pieces from decorative paper. Be sure to use a sturdier paper stock for the bow tie and nose.

9 Using the templates, cut 2 rabbit ears out of felt. With each ear, fold the bottom edges in toward the center to add dimension. Use a stapler to keep the ears folded.

10 Adhere the veneer to the embroidery hoop using tacky glue. Flip the hoop over so the veneer side is on the bottom. Push the cardboard support firmly into the back of the hoop. It should fit snugly. Weight the hoop and let dry completely.

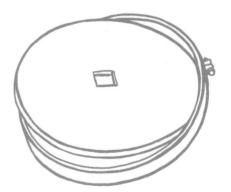

11 Once dry, flip the hoop over. Orient the hoop so that the embroidery hoop screw mechanism sits at the bottom edge of the clock, where it will be hidden by the bow tie. Coat the wood veneer clock face evenly with decoupage glue and apply the paper eyes, cheeks, and bow tie. Once dry, staple the ears to the back of the hoop.

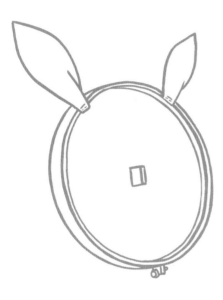

12 Once dry, insert the clock mechanism. To finish, glue the nose to the top of the clock mechanism with the strong glue. Make sure there is enough glue to secure the nose, but not so much that it will run down beyond the tip of the mechanism.

13 Hang to the wall on a nail.

14 See time go by!

tips

▶ By changing ear shapes and accessories you can change this clock into another animal.

▶ Every nursery needs a clock, but this will make a great gift for a kid of any age.

GAME TIME

play table

LEVEL: ◻ **FINISHED MEASUREMENTS:** 16" X 30" X 30" (40.5CM X 76CM X 76CM)

MATERIALS

- One 30" x 30" (76cm x 76cm) piece of ¾"- (2cm-) thick plywood board, preferably high-quality, such as maple-apple 12-ply
- four 16" (40.5cm) wooden legs
- carpenter's wood glue
- decoupage glue
- large scrap paper, such as a brown grocery bag or butcher paper
- large sheets of assorted heavyweight colored and patterned papers (i.e., wall paper, thicker wrapping paper, etc.)
- water-based polyurethane varnish

TOOLS

- sandpaper
- drill with bits
- medium 3" (7.5cm) flat paintbrush
- 10" (25.5cm) dinner plate
- pencil
- large straightedge or ruler
- scissors
- measuring tape
- wide flat paintbrush
- small 1" (2.5cm) flat paintbrush

Finger painting, Valentine writing, puzzle building, and crafting galore; every kid needs a special table just their size. This handsome mid-century–inspired piece is so attractive, it may even earn a spot in your family living room.

instructions

1. Sand the edges and surface of the plywood piece so that it is smooth. Wipe off any dust. Decide which side you want to use for the top of the table and lay your board face down on the floor or a flat work surface.

2. Drill holes for each of the wooden legs 2" (5cm) in from each corner. Add wood glue to the base of each leg, where it will meet the table. Screw the legs in securely.

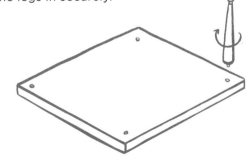

3 Flip the table over.

4 Coat the entire surface of the tabletop with decoupage glue and allow to dry. While it is drying, select your papers.

5 To build your template: Take the dinner plate and trace its circumference onto the scrap paper using a pencil. Measure 7" (18cm) away from the edge of the circle and make a small dot. Draw straight lines from the dot back to the edge of the circle, forming a teardrop shape. Cut this shape out, fold it in half, and cut on the fold line. This will be your template. Using the template, cut out pieces from the decorative papers to make four large teardrops.

6 Find the exact center of the table surface and make a small mark. Lay out your paper pieces with the teardrop points meeting at the tabletop's center mark. One piece at a time, apply the pieces to the table surface using a medium to large size brush to coat it with decoupage glue. Allow to dry. Coat the entire surface of the tabletop with decoupage glue again to ensure that all the paper is sealed. Allow to dry.

7 Choose a well-ventilated place for this step, far from kids and pets. Using a wide brush, apply one to two coats of polyurethane varnish, waiting for it to dry in between coats. This will protect the surface of your table and will make it easier to clean. Coat the edges of the table with one coat using a small brush.

8 Let the games begin!

tips

▶ You can use the same technique and design and upcycle a coffee table, if you don't want to build a table from scratch. Be mindful of the table's height and the age of the little ones meant to use it, so they can sit comfortably.

▶ Customize the colors of your papers, or paint the wood a solid color before starting, if you prefer. If you do so, allow 24 hours for the paint to dry and settle before you start decoupaging.

▶ For a different look, you can purchase or repurpose hairpin legs instead of wooden ones.

ONCE UPON A TIME book ledges

MATERIALS

- ▶ Letters templates (page 128)
- ▶ artist tape
- ▶ three 24"- (61cm-) long pieces of a 2x2 strip of wood (note that a 2x2 piece of wood has an approximate dimension of 1.5" x 1.5" [3.8cm x 3.8cm])
- ▶ 3"- (7.5cm-) long screws, appropriate to your wall type
- ▶ three 24" (61cm) pieces of 3"- (7.5cm-) wide and ¼"- (6mm-) thick basswood for the front of the shelves
- ▶ decoupage glue
- ▶ various colored or patterned papers
- ▶ carpenter's wood glue

TOOLS

- ▶ measuring tape
- ▶ level
- ▶ pencil
- ▶ drill with bits
- ▶ scissors
- ▶ medium 3" (7.5cm) flat paintbrush

LEVEL: **FINISHED MEASUREMENTS:** 3" X 24" X 1¾" (7.5CM X 61CM X 4.5CM) PER LEDGE

You can absolutely judge a book by its cover. Kids love to pick their story time favorites and find their beloved books at first sight. This project is very fast and affordable. It makes a fun ever-changing display in a child's room while still being super practical.

instructions

1. Determine where on the wall you would like your three book ledges. If you are using them for board books or picture books, use one of the taller books to calculate the ideal distance in between the ledges. I hung my shelves 13" (33cm) apart measuring from the bottom of one shelf to the bottom of the next shelf.

2. Use artist tape to mark where each shelf should be. Using the level, make a straight vertical line with tape to serve as a guide against which you can line up all the shelves vertically.

ONCE

6 Use carpenter's wood glue to adhere the basswood pieces to the front of each of the 2x2s. Use artist tape to wrap the edges of each shelf in order to prevent the basswood front piece from sliding while the glue is drying. Allow it to dry overnight so the wood pieces are completely bonded. Remove tape.

3 Working one at a time, screw the wood 2x2s into the wall following the tape guides. Use three screws to secure each piece of wood to the wall.

7 Story time!

4 Coat one side of each of the three basswood pieces with decoupage glue. Allow to dry.

5 Using the Letters templates, enlarged 200 percent, cut out the phrase "Once Upon a Time" or any phrase of your choosing from the decorative papers. Adhere the paper letters to the pieces of basswood with decoupage glue. Coat with a final layer of decoupage glue.

tips

▶ You can repurpose old wood for this project as long as you find an evenly square piece to be the ledge and a flat piece to be the front.

▶ Rotate the offerings in this library by switching up books once a week, and choose some new favorites for the week to come.

ABC

San Francisco

#062

In My Nest

Now I Am BIG!

CAN FLY

ON

PRESS
●
HERE

You Are My Baby FARM

You Are My Baby

spinach ravioli

T turkey burgers
W pan fried fish + salad
T italian meatballs
F fish tacos
S pizza night!
S braised shortribs

2

FAMILY LIFE

This chapter aims to bring handmade, practical, and fun ideas to every room in the house. With an eye for simplifying and improving daily routines, most of these projects offer useful yet visually interesting results, sure to spruce up any family kitchen, entryway, or dining room.

I've included a child-friendly coat rack that helps get coats off the floor, an adhesive chalkboard tree for organizing family messages and notes, a dry-erase dinner menu planner that I use every weekend to plan meals for the week ahead, and a step stool to welcome little helpers in the kitchen.

As with many projects in the book, this chapter encourages you to make these items your own, allowing you to change the colors or the sizes to fit perfectly with your space and your family lifestyle.

LEAF A MESSAGE family memo board

MATERIALS

- roll of chalkboard contact paper 18" (45.5cm) wide
- artist tape
- six 7" (18cm) round cork trivets
- assorted colored or patterned paper
- six 2"-3" (5cm-7.5cm) screws to hang trivets on wall
- decoupage glue
- chalk

TOOLS

- multipurpose spray adhesive
- scissors
- large ruler
- level
- measuring tape
- pencil

LEVEL: ☐   **FINISHED MEASUREMENTS:** 45" X 34" (114CM X 86CM)

Organization and communication is a big key to the happy family. There are so many moving parts to our days that having an eye-catching system to keep the essentials in one place will help make your life a little easier. And the chalkboard panels give creative kids license to write on the wall, without making a mess. Bonus!

instructions

1. Using scissors, cut out the following pieces of chalkboard contact paper: one 36" x 8" (91cm x 20.5cm) piece, five 20" x 2" (51cm x 5cm) pieces, and seven 10" x 2" (25.5cm x 5cm) pieces. The largest piece will be the trunk. Set this aside.

2. The smaller pieces are the branches. These will need to be cut at 45-degree angles where they meet each other or the trunk piece. I recommend that you first lay out the branch pieces on the

pieces one by one, and firmly adhere the pieces to the wall. Smooth them down with the palm of your hand.

6 Using the cork trivets as a guide, cut matching paper circles from any decorative paper you choose.

7 Mount the trivets among the tree branches using a screw at the center of the circle. Use spray adhesive to adhere the decorative paper circles to the front of the trivet boards. The screws are now perfectly concealed.

8 Grab the chalk and start writing!

floor in the configuration you desire before cutting the angle. This will help you determine the direction of your angled cut.

3 Before permanently adhering the tree pieces to the wall, I highly recommend that you first position the pieces as desired using loops of artist tape to quickly mount them to the wall. Start with the trunk, then add the branches.

4 Use a level to ensure that the trunk is perfectly straight.

5 Once everything looks good, remove the backing from the contact paper

tips

▶ You can also decorate your tree with chalkboard leaves for additional room for family reminders, events, and announcements.

▶ Rather than using patterned paper for the bird growth chart, try using chalkboard contact paper. Hang in playrooms, kids' rooms, and nurseries and have your kids customize!

WHAT'S COOKING?

dry-erase dinner planner

MATERIALS

- Letters templates (page 128)
- 14" x 11" x 1½" (35.5 x 28cm x 3.8cm) picture frame with glass
- various colored and patterned papers
- double-sided tape
- Clear Gel tacky glue
- two small Mighty Magnets
- dry-erase marker

TOOLS

- craft knife or scissors
- cutting mat
- large ruler

LEVEL: ☐   **FINISHED MEASUREMENTS:** 14" X 11" X 1½" (35.5 X 28CM X 3.8CM)

Nothing makes me sadder than overripe produce or a spoiled bunch of broccoli on its way to the compost bin, victim of my lack of better meal planning. I've been daydreaming about an easy-to-use dinner planner, and voilà, here it is, dry-erase et al. May the next broccoli find itself to a happy tummy and befriend some pasta on the way.

instructions

1. Using a craft knife or scissors, cut out seven 2" x 11" (5cm x 28cm) strips of paper. Choose papers that are not too heavily patterned or dark. You want your writing to be legible once the board is assembled.

2. Using the Letters templates, enlarged 150 percent, cut out the first letter of the days of the week from a solid colored paper.

6 Place the board into the frame and reassemble the frame back.

7 Using tacky glue, adhere one of the magnets to the top of the frame, and the other to the dry-erase marker to always keep it handy.

8 Start menu planning!

3 Lay out your paper strips vertically in an appealing order.

4 Use the cardboard or mat board backing that came with the frame and adhere the strips of paper to it using double-sided tape.

5 Once these are all in place, use double-sided tape to adhere the paper letters for the days of the week along the left side of the board. Make sure to leave enough room on the left edge of the board so the letters will not be covered by the frame once the board is placed in the frame.

tips

▶ This project can be easily scaled up to accommodate more meals or days. Be creative!

▶ If you want to keep it simple, alternate two different types or colors of paper.

▶ Adhere the Mighty Magnet to the dry-erase marker cap; that way once you need to replace the marker, you can keep the magnetized cap. Cover with paper to customize.

M spinach ravioli

T turkey burger

W pan fried fish + salad

T italian meatballs

F fish tacos

S pizza night !

S braised shortribs

1 Litro

2 8

I SEE YOU

window film cutouts

MATERIALS

- **Window Film Cutouts templates (pages 138–139)**
- **etched-glass window film**

TOOLS

- **craft knife or scissors**
- **cutting mat**
- **¼" (6mm) hole punch**
- **ruler**
- **spray bottle**

LEVEL: ☐ **FINISHED MEASUREMENTS:** 16" X 22" (40.5CM X 56CM)

This is a fun and super fast project—whether you want a bit of privacy, need to spruce up a not-so-fantastic view, or are just naturally inclined to live in spring all year round.

instructions

1. Using the templates, cut out one starburst flower, two tulip flowers, one dotted flower, twelve almond leaves, five drop leaf, and one flower centerpiece from the window film. The window film has an opaque backing, which should not be removed until the pieces are cut. For the largest flower, keep in mind that the starburst-shaped center piece that you'll be cutting out will also be used in the scene, so cut carefully.

2. Cut ¼"- (6mm-) wide strips of window film for the stems. You will need two 6"- (15cm-) long strips, two 8"- (20.5cm-) long strips, and one 10"- (25.5cm-) long strip.

3 Once all the pieces are cut, clean your window thoroughly. The window film will only adhere to a smooth, clean glass surface.

4 Spray the glass with a small amount of water and apply the window film, smoothing it down with the flat of your hand. Space the flower stems roughly 4-5″ apart. Make sure none of your pieces overlap, as they will not stick to one another.

5 Enjoy the view!

tips

▶ Make sure you are using a window film that clings to the glass without an adhesive. A clinging window film is easy to remove and reposition and is best suited to this project.

▶ Cut as many additional pieces as you would like to expand the size of your scene.

▶ You can freestyle a few birds, bugs, or even your entire design!

▶ With this fast, easy-to-remove technique you can decorate other glass items, such as mirrors, or you can use it for holiday or party decor.

▶ KID FUN

FLOWER GARDEN NOTECARDS

A number of the templates provided in this book can double as great coloring pages and art activities. Use a copy of the Window Film Cutouts template, and have your child create fun notecards. Depending on age, encourage your child to simply color the design with crayons or for a more challenging activity, collage or paint on them.

NEW HEIGHTS

step stool

LEVEL: ☐   **FINISHED MEASUREMENTS:** APPLE BOX IS 8" X 12" X 10"(20.5CM X 30.5CM X 25.5CM)

MATERIALS

- ▶ **Step Stool templates (page 140)**
- ▶ **8"- (20.5cm-) tall apple box**
- ▶ **decoupage glue**
- ▶ **assorted colored and patterned papers**
- ▶ **assorted found papers**
- ▶ **water-based polyurethane varnish**
- ▶ **rubber or cork adhesive dots (optional)**

TOOLS

- ▶ **1"–3" (2.5cm–7.5cm) paintbrush**
- ▶ **scissors**
- ▶ **measuring tape or large ruler**

I'm the faint-of-heart type of mama and when a toddler's mighty powers know no boundaries or height limitations, I worry! I found the sturdiest and biggest of step stools: An apple box is a wooden box or crate used by film crews and photographers everywhere! Since my little one has always been our assistant chef, I designed this apple template to make this handy stool become a prettier addition to our kitchen landscape. Confession: I use it, too!

instructions

1 Using a paintbrush, coat the side of the apple box to be decorated with decoupage glue. Allow to dry.

2 Using the templates, cut out 3 apple lefts, 2 apple rights, 1 apple bitten, 6 apple leafs, and 3 apple stem pieces from any papers you choose.

3. Measure the box horizontally to find the center point. With the point as your guide, apply the center apple piece and brush with decoupage glue. Apply and brush the remaining paper pieces. Allow to dry.

4. Apply a final coat of decoupage glue all over the entire surface. Allow to dry completely. Overnight is recommended.

5. To protect the stool, coat the entire box with polyurethane. Let dry for 2 hours. Repeat.

6. Step on it! It's sturdy enough for the whole family to enjoy. Hello, lost teapot on top shelf!

tips

▶ Customize this step stool to your heart's desire. Many other templates in the book will work well here, including the bird from page 133, the owl from page 132, or personalize it with a name using the letters on page 128.

▶ If your floors are particularly slippery or if you want extra grip, add rubber or cork dots to the bottom corners of the stool.

ALL ABOUT ME memory box

MATERIALS

▶ Memory Box templates (page 141)

▶ Letters templates (page 128)

▶ decoupage glue

▶ 2½" x 9" x 12" (6.5cm x 23cm x 30.5cm) wooden box

▶ assorted colored or patterned papers, the more graphic the better

▶ 4" x 4" (10cm x 10cm) photo

▶ artist tape

TOOLS

▶ scissors

▶ binder clips (optional)

▶ craft knife

▶ 1"–3" (2.5cm–7.5cm) flat paintbrush

LEVEL: ☐   **FINISHED MEASUREMENTS:** 2½" X 9" X 12" (6.5CM X 23CM X 30.5CM)

There are traditional baby keepsakes, like footprints, ultrasounds, hair locks, and itsy-bitsy booties. And less traditional momentos, such as newspaper clippings from the baby's birth date, tickets to the concert where the parents met, or even a food label from something mom craved during pregnancy. No matter what you choose, this is your catchall box. Warning: Heart melting will occur when box is reopened after a few years.

instructions

1 Using the templates, cut out 1 sun ring and 16 sun rays from any papers you choose. I use binder clips to hold the template to the decorative paper for easier precision when cutting.

2 Brush an even coat of decoupage glue on the box lid and set aside to dry.

3. Using the template as a guide, cut the photograph into a circle shape matching the inner edge of the sun ring.

4. Brush decoupage glue onto the lid and apply the sun ring and photo to the box. Apply another coat of decoupage glue on the sun ring and then add the sun rays.

5. Using the Letters templates, enlarged if desired, cut out the initials you would like from any paper you choose. Mark an even line on the box lid with artist tape. Apply an even coat of decoupage glue above the tape and apply your paper letters. Set aside to dry.

6. Apply a final coat of decoupage glue to the entire box lid.

7. Smile. It is adorable, right?

tips

▶ You may choose to spell a baby's first name, instead of the initials, with the Letters templates provided on page 128.

▶ Test the decoupage glue on a corner of the photo to make sure it doesn't darken or bleed, not all photo paper will react the same.

▶ If you are the "collector" type and have heaps of saved mementos, you can either choose a bigger box, or do several, and number them.

▶ KID FUN

COLLAGE ART

Recycle a wood board or choose thick cardstock as the canvas for children to create their own masterpieces.

Have preschool-aged children use child safety scissors to cut colored pattern papers to their liking. Pour a small amount of decoupage glue in small bowl or lid. Dip a small flat brush in the glue and cover a section of the canvas surface. Glue the papers to this surface. When the masterpiece is ready and dry, cover with a last coat of decoupage glue.

For older children, you can encourage them to create a shape with the cutouts instead of an abstract creation, for an extra challenge.

MASTERPIECES

family gallery

MATERIALS

▶ **Homasote board, cut to fit your wall space**

▶ **wallpaper, approximately 2"–3" (5cm–7.5cm) larger than the board**

▶ **multipurpose spray adhesive**

▶ **two 3" (7.5cm) bulldog clips**

▶ **two 1" (2.5cm) screws**

▶ **two oversized rubber bands**

▶ **four screws appropriate for your wall and washers to size**

▶ **thumbtacks**

TOOLS

▶ **staple gun and staples**

LEVEL: ☐ **FINISHED MEASUREMENTS:** VARIES, SAMPLE PHOTOGRAPHED IS 12" X 48" (30.5CM X 122CM)

This project was inspired by the endless influx of my kid's art and craft projects, family snapshots, and loved pieces of memories that I wanted to display. This board can live in any room in the house, and can be adapted in size to your space and need.

instructions

1. At the home improvement store or lumber yard, have your Homasote board cut to the size you desire.

2. Cut a sheet of wallpaper that is 2"–3" (5cm–7.5cm) larger than the board. Lay it face down on the ground.

3. Take the board outside or to a well-ventilated area and cover one side of it with multipurpose spray adhesive.

6. Measure 3" (7.5cm) from the right edge of the board for the first bulldog clip, and 12" (30.5cm) for the second one. Both should be 2" (5cm) from top of board. Use the two 1" (2.5cm) screws to affix the bulldog clips to the Homasote board.

7. Slide the rubber bands onto the other end of the board.

8. Using screws that are appropriate to your wall, and washers to size, screw the board to the wall, one screw in each of the four corners.

4. Lay the board, adhesive side down and centered, on top of the paper. Flip the paper-covered board over briefly to make sure there are no bumps or wrinkles in the paper. Smooth out any imperfections and flip the board back over.

9. Sort through piles of art and photos and pick some winners. Rotate to your liking!

5. Pull the wallpaper taut over the sides of the board, stapling as you go. At the corners, fold the edges of paper neatly as you would when wrapping a present. Staple the folds into place. Once the wallpaper is firmly secured, flip the board over.

tips

▶ This project can also work well with fabric instead of wallpaper.

▶ You can customize the number and location of the clips or rubber bands to the size of artwork or future use of the board.

HANG TOGETHER friends coat rack

LEVEL: ☐ **FINISHED MEASUREMENTS:** 8" X 24" X ¾" (20.5CM X 61CM X 2CM)

MATERIALS

- **Friends Coat Rack templates (pages 142–45)**
- **8" x 24" (20.5cm x 61cm) piece of ¾"- (2cm-) thick plywood board**
- **decoupage glue**
- **assorted colored and patterned papers**
- **assorted found papers**
- **four 3" (7.5cm) screws that work with the wall anchors**
- **three wood knobs, 1½" (3.8cm) in diameter**
- **wall anchors appropriate for your wall type**

TOOLS

- **sandpaper**
- **dry brush or tack cloth**
- **1"–3" (2.5cm–7.5cm) flat paintbrush**
- **binder clips (optional)**
- **¼" (6mm) hole punch**
- **¾" (2cm) hole punch**
- **scissors**
- **pencil**
- **ruler**
- **drill with bits**
- **level (optional)**

This project lives at the intersection of cute and functional. I love surrounding my family with witty and fun objects that we can use daily. I guarantee this will produce a smile from any little one if you hang these friendly faces within their reach.

instructions

1. Sand any rough edges that may be on the plywood board. Remove all sawdust with a dry brush.

2. Apply an even coat of decoupage glue on one side of the board. Allow to dry.

3. Using the templates, cut out the bear, rabbit, and fox pieces from any decorative papers you chose. Use the ¼" (6mm) hole punch to create the six animal eyes using a dark piece of paper for contrast. Use the ¾" (2cm) hole punch to cut two circles for the fox cheeks.

4 To apply the animal faces, first measure the board to find its center and make a small mark in pencil.

5 Start with the middle animal (fox), using your mark as a guide for the center of the fox head. Brush an even coat of decoupage glue on the board and apply the fox head piece, followed by the fox muzzle piece, brushing over each piece with an even coat of decoupage glue as you go. Complete the two remaining animal faces in the same way. Allow to dry.

6 Apply a final coat of decoupage glue over the entire surface of the board. Allow to dry overnight or until completely dry.

7 To create holes for the mounting screws, drill a hole in each corner of the board, measuring ¾" (2cm) in from each side.

8 Mark the holes for the knobs with pencil before drilling to ensure that the knobs are just where you want them, following the template. Once the holes are drilled, screw in the knobs.

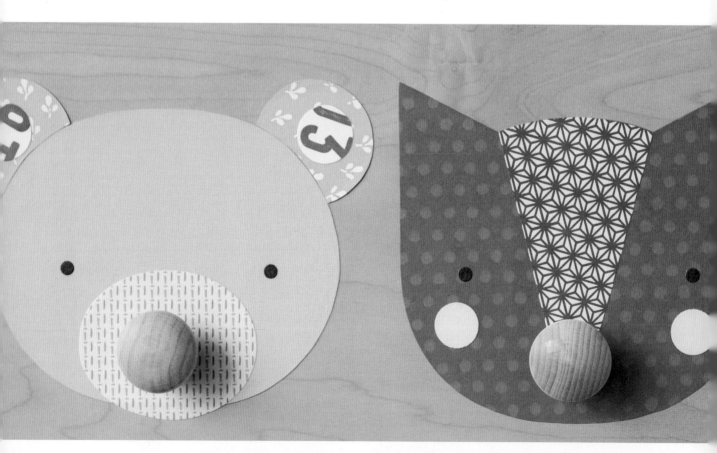

9. Position the coat rack on your wall. Remember to hang it within kids' reach. Mark the placement. Use a level if necessary. Find wall anchors that are appropriate for your type of wall. If possible, find a stud on one side. Once you install the anchors, screw the coat rack hanger onto the wall.

10. Just like magic, see those scarfs, hats, and coats stay off the floor.

tips

▶ If you have a Goldilocks fan, the animal faces could easily become three little bears.

▶ Vintage knobs of different sizes can be found in flea markets and building reuse centers. Using upcycled materials gives the piece a different feel.

▶ Alternatively, you can add picture hanging hardware to the back of the coat rack in order to conceal the screws.

▶ KID FUN

COLOR IT YOURSELF ANIMAL STICKERS

Make an extra copy of the Friends Coat Rack templates on pages 142–45. Have kids color and decorate the animal faces.

For extra fun, apply double-sided tape, adhesive dots, or a double-sided repositionable adhesive sheet to the back of the final decorated animal faces sheet, then cut out each animal face for easy and fab new stickers!

LIGHT THE WAY ceiling pendant

LEVEL: ☐ **FINISHED MEASUREMENTS:** 13" X 8" X 8" (33CM X 20.5CM X 20.5CM)

MATERIALS

- ▶ **Ceiling Pendant templates (pages 146-47)**
- ▶ **14-ply chipboard**
- ▶ **2"- (5cm-) wide gummed paper tape**
- ▶ **assorted colored papers**
- ▶ **assorted found papers**
- ▶ **decoupage glue**
- ▶ **cord kit**
- ▶ **CFL bulb**

TOOLS

- ▶ **scissors**
- ▶ **craft knife or utility knife**
- ▶ **cutting mat**
- ▶ **1"-3" (2.5cm-7.5cm) flat paintbrush**

Lamps are great accents to add character to a room. Designed to go in any space in the contemporary family home, this mod-house ceiling pendant is sure to be noticed.

instructions

1. Using the templates enlarged 200 percent and either a craft knife or a utility knife, cut out 2 lamp sides with star shape, 2 lamp sides without star shape, 1 lamp interior panel, and 4 lamp tops from the chipboard. Precision is very important for this project.

2. Cut two 7"- (18cm-) long strips of the gummed tape, and four 8"- (20.5cm-) long strips. Cut each of these strips down the center, making 1"- (92.5cm-) wide strips of tape. To use gummed tape, flip the tape shiny side up, and brush with water. The shiny side is now an active adhesive.

3. Construct the pyramid-shaped "roof" of the

lamp, using the 7" (18cm) gummed tape pieces to hold the 4 lamp top pieces together. Set aside to dry.

4 Now construct the rectangular base with four of the eight 8" (20.5cm) strips of tape, making sure the lamp sides with the star shape are opposite each other. Set aside to dry.

5 Sit the "roof" on top of the rectangular base and connect using the remaining four of the gummed tape pieces. Allow to dry completely.

6 Using the templates, cut out 4 large decorative triangles and 12 small decorative triangles from any colored or found papers you choose. Apply the paper triangles using decoupage glue, brushing the entire exterior surface of the lamp as you go.

7 To assemble the lamp, thread the cord of the cord kit through the interior panel piece and then upward through the lamp shade. Screw in the bulb and it's ready to use.

8 Let there be light!

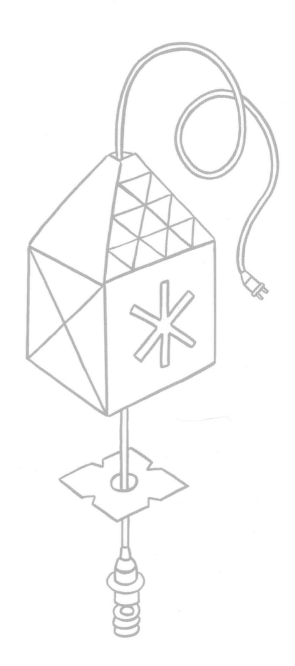

▶ You can transform this project for a traditional little girl's room. Think scallops, flowers, and maybe even use the shape to create a little house. But if you are going this route, please add something unexpected, like some fluorescent pink!

▶ Make sure to use a CFL or low-temperature light bulb.

3
PLAYTIME

I'm a firm believer that some of the best gifts for kids to develop their creativity are toys, and if the toy is handmade and unique, that is even better. In this chapter you will find great play time projects for girls and boys, and children big or small. There are custom baby blocks that are sure to be a baby shower hit, a peekaboo house that will entertain toddlers for hours, and re-envisioned classics such as a portable doll house or a colorful drum, and animals masks for the preschooler set.

Whether you simply customize these projects using a child's favorite color (instead of red, why not a purple drum), or let your imagination soar and transform the doll house into a magic castle, or a car wash, I'm sure you will find smiles and endless hours of imaginary play the result of any variation of the project ideas here. And that, in return, is the best gift for you.

FROM THE GROUND UP

custom baby blocks

MATERIALS

- ▶ **Custom Baby Blocks templates (pages 148–49)**
- ▶ **Letters templates (page 128)**
- ▶ **Numbers templates (page 129)**
- ▶ **four or more 2½" x 2½" x 2½" (6.5cm x 6.5cm x 6.5cm) unfinished wood blocks (at least as many as there are letters in the child's name)**
- ▶ **decoupage glue**
- ▶ **assorted colored and patterned papers**
- ▶ **assorted found papers**

TOOLS

- ▶ **sandpaper**
- ▶ **1"–3" (2.5cm–7.5cm) flat paintbrush**
- ▶ **craft knife**
- ▶ **cutting mat**
- ▶ **scissors**

LEVEL: ☐   **FINISHED MEASUREMENTS:** 2½" X 2½" X 2½" (6.5CM X 6.5CM X 6.5CM) BLOCKS

These keepsake blocks are lovely for play and display. Spelling the child's name is an extra special touch. Playful motifs from our collection give this classic toy a modern spin.

instructions

1. Gently sand away any rough edges from the wood blocks.

2. Coat the exterior of each block with decoupage glue. Allow to dry.

3. Using the templates, cut out all apple, bird, boat, crown, heart, tree, sun, and clover pieces from any decorative papers you choose. Make sure to mix and match papers and colors.

4. Using the Letters templates, cut out the letters of baby's name from any decorative papers you choose.

5　Using the Numbers templates, cut out number pieces from any decorative papers you choose. Include a number for each block being made.

6　Apply the paper shapes and letters to the blocks using decoupage glue. Allow to dry.

7　Apply a final protective coat of decoupage glue to the entire surface of the blocks. Allow to dry.

8　Spell your name!

tips

▶ You can customize the icons and colors to a room theme.

▶ If you want to make a full set of blocks, spell out the child's first, middle, and last name.

ROAR!

animal masks

MATERIALS

- ▶ Animal Masks templates (pages 150–53)
- ▶ thin new or repurposed cardboard (such as a cereal box)
- ▶ assorted colored or patterned papers
- ▶ decoupage glue
- ▶ elastic string or ribbon

TOOLS

- ▶ scissors
- ▶ 1"–3" (2.5cm–7.5cm) flat paintbrush
- ▶ cutting mat
- ▶ ruler or straightedge
- ▶ bone folder
- ▶ craft knife
- ▶ pencil
- ▶ ¼" (6mm) hole punch or large needle

LEVEL: ☐   **FINISHED MEASUREMENTS:** OWL: 4½" X 7" (11CM X 18CM); TIGER: 6½" X 8" (16.5CM X 20.5CM)

Let your own wild things show you their roars with these easy-to-make masks. They can even help you create them. As my kid says: Don't be scared! It's pretend!

instructions

1. Begin constructing the mask pieces with the animal head templates. Select paper for the tiger head and the owl face. Using the templates for the tiger head and the owl face, cut out a piece of cardboard roughly the same outline. Coat each cardboard piece with decoupage glue and lay face down on the back of the chosen papers. Smooth it out with your hand and allow them to dry under a weight. Set aside.

2. Using the templates, cut out the remaining animal pieces from the decorative papers you choose. Pick a sturdy paper for the tiger ears, tiger snout, and owl beak pieces. Crease the beak and snout pieces according to the templates. To

do so, lay the corresponding template over the snout or beak piece. Set a ruler or straightedge on the crease lines and run a bone folder along the lines. These lines will transfer to the pieces below. Set aside.

③ Cut the eye holes out of the tiger head, owl face, and owl eyes pieces using a craft knife. Apply the remaining pieces using decoupage glue.

④ For the tiger snout: Fold the flaps back from the center triangle of the tiger's nose. Using decoupage glue, adhere the angled tabs together, forming the three-dimensional snout. The tabs at the base of the snout should be folded inward and will be hidden. Apply glue

to these tabs and adhere the snout to the tiger's face.

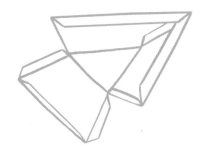

⑤ For the owl beak: Fold backward away from the center diamond shape. Apply glue to the angled tabs and adhere the beak to the owl's face.

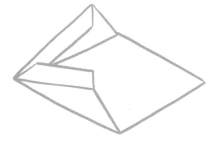

MAKE YOUR OWN ANIMAL

Choose a basic Animal Mask template on pages 150–53. Use the template and cut the mask from a piece of cardstock .

Ask children to imagine the animal they want to be or look up a photograph of their favorite animal, and help them design the fun characteristics that bring this animal mask to life. They can choose the animal color, coloring in stripes or spots, make ears with different papers, whiskers with string, and draw, paint, and collage in the details.

6. Once dry, use the hole punch to poke holes for the elastic string or ribbon, using the template as a visual guide.

7. Thread the string through, leaving enough extra to knot.

8. Let the wild rumpus begin. Hear them roar and hoot!

tips

▶ This is a great party activity to do with kids. If you prepare the cut out pieces ahead of time, they will enjoy designing and creating their own unique masks.

▶ The same technique can be used to make other animals.

RAT-A-TAT-TAT toy drum

LEVEL: ☒ FINISHED MEASUREMENTS: VARIES
DEPENDING ON THE TIN CONTAINER

MATERIALS

- ▶ Toy Drum template (page 154)
- ▶ large round tin container
- ▶ spray or acrylic paint (optional)
- ▶ wallpaper scrap big enough to wrap around the container
- ▶ decoupage glue
- ▶ 2 brass fasteners
- ▶ assorted colored and patterned papers
- ▶ assorted found papers
- ▶ artist tape
- ▶ 32"- (81cm-) long, thin leather belt or trim
- ▶ colored felt for the drum top
- ▶ Clear Gel tacky glue
- ▶ two 12"- (30.5cm-) long round wood dowels
- ▶ two spherical wood beads with holes large enough to insert the dowels
- ▶ carpenter's wood glue

TOOLS

- ▶ ruler or measuring tape
- ▶ scissors
- ▶ 1"–3" (2.5cm–7.5cm) flat paintbrush
- ▶ pencil
- ▶ hammer and nail or drill
- ▶ cutting mat
- ▶ craft knife
- ▶ leather hole punch (optional)

A big cookie tin may have initially said "yummy" to you, but it will definitely say "noisy" in its second life. This project requires very few skills to make, but will receive a cheerful standing ovation—or better yet, a well-deserved drum roll.

instructions

1. Depending on your found container, you may want to first paint it using either spray paint or acrylic paint. If you choose to do this, paint the lid and container separately.

2. Start by measuring the height of the container. Cut a strip of wallpaper that is long enough to wrap around the circumference of the container. Adhere the wallpaper to the tin using decoupage glue. Allow to dry.

3. Determine where you would like the strap to be attached. Mark two holes roughly 1½" (3.8cm) below the top of the container. Ideally, you

want to measure the circumference of the drum, divide by three, and mark two of those three measurements for placement of the strap. This way the straps end up closer to the child and won't interfere with drum playing. Punch holes into the tin container where you have marked using either a nail and hammer or a drill. The holes should be large enough for the arms of the brass fasteners to pass through.

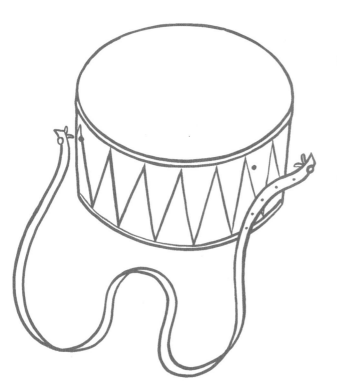

4　Using the template, cut out 12 to 16 drum triangle pieces from the decorative papers you chose. Feel free to adjust the template to the specifics of your container. I recommend that you temporarily adhere the paper pieces to the container using small loops of artist tape. This will give you a chance to determine how to space out and arrange the pieces. Don't worry about the triangles meeting perfectly corner to corner. Adjust the quantity of triangle pieces as desired.

5　Once the pieces are arranged, adhere them one by one to the drum using decoupage glue. Coat the entire collaged area with a final coat of decoupage glue. Allow to dry.

6　Cut the leather belt down to 32" (81cm). Using a craft knife, cut a small slit at either end of the belt (or cut several on one side if you wish to accommodate different aged children. You may be able to use one of the existing belt holes. This will be your drum strap. Attach the strap to the drum using the brass fasteners.

7 Put the lid on, and touch up the paint if necessary.

8 Top the drum with a circle of brightly colored felt. To make: Use the lid as a template, then cut out a felt circle ½" (13mm) smaller all the way around. Adhere the felt with tacky glue.

9 For the drumsticks: Attach wood beads to dowels with carpenter's wood glue. Allow to dry completely.

10 Music, please!

tips

▶ You can use different sizes of cookie tins, smaller ones may look particularly charming.

▶ Alternatively, you can use a round cardboard box, such as a hat box. Just make sure the drum sound is to your liking before you start crafting.

ALL IN THE FAMILY memory game

MATERIALS

- 4 sheets of 8½ x 11" (21.5cm x 28cm) patterned cardstock
- double-sided repositionable adhesive sheets
- twelve 3" x 3" (7.5cm x 7.5cm) photos of family members, each printed twice
- round 3"- (7.5cm-) diameter tin or other small keepsake box

TOOLS

- scissors
- 2½" (6.5cm) hole punch

LEVEL: ○ **FINISHED MEASUREMENTS:** 2½" (6.5CM) RADIUS

The rewarding moment of finding a matching card pairing reaches sky-high happiness when the image on the card is of a favorite auntie or cousin! Our family is spread around the globe, so I designed this game to keep all their faces familiar to my toddler. It works great as flashcards for wee ones, too.

instructions

1. Pick a fun, colorful patterned paper. I used cardstock that I stamped using the eraser on the end of a pencil (see page 20).

2. Print out or photocopy the photos of your family members at a size so their faces can fit comfortably within a 2½" (6.5cm) circle. A good size for the overall print would be a 3" x 3" (7.5cm x 7.5cm) square. Print two copies of each portrait. Cut out each image roughly, leaving plenty of space around the border.

3 Using double-sided repositionable adhesive sheets, remove one side of the paper covering and apply it to the back of the patterned paper. Peel away the other side of the adhesive sheet and lay the photos face up onto the exposed adhesive. This may take several sheets, depending on the size of the patterned paper and the quantity of your photos.

4 Punch out the photos using the 2½" (6.5cm) hole punch. I recommend laying the photo side face down so that it is visible through the puncher window before you punch. This way you can center the image. Do this with the 24 pieces.

5 Store the completed memory game pieces in a tin. You can decorate the tin with the same pattern as the cardstock.

6 Let the games begin!

tips

▶ This project would be fun using classmates instead of family members.

▶ For the tin I used a candy tin, but any round containers can work, such as the ones used for spices or office supplies.

MI CASA ES SU CASA

portable dollhouse

LEVEL: **FINISHED MEASUREMENTS:** 14" X 20" X 20" (35.5CM X 51CM X 51CM)

MATERIALS

- ▶ two 14" x 20" (35.5cm x 51cm) pieces of 14-ply chipboard
- ▶ birch wood veneer sheets
- ▶ 4 sheets assorted wallpapers
- ▶ mounting spray
- ▶ 2"- (5cm-) wide gummed paper tape
- ▶ scrap paper and cardboard

TOOLS

- ▶ ruler
- ▶ pencil
- ▶ utility knife
- ▶ cutting mat
- ▶ small brush

If there was a way of counting the number of hours I spent in my childhood playing with dolls and my dollhouse, I'm pretty sure it would prove to be rather astonishing. I used spools for tables, my sneakers became cars, and for a while I looked at everything for its potential of becoming dollhouse furnishings. This nifty paper construction will easily be the happiest house on the block. It folds up for easy portability.

instructions

1. Cut two pieces of chipboard measuring 14" x 20" (35.5cm x 51cm). On each piece: Measure 10" (25.5cm) up on both sides. Mark with pencil. Find center on the top edge. Mark with pencil. Draw a line from each 10" (25.5cm) mark up to the top center. These two lines will form the peak of the roof. Cut on the lines to create a peak.

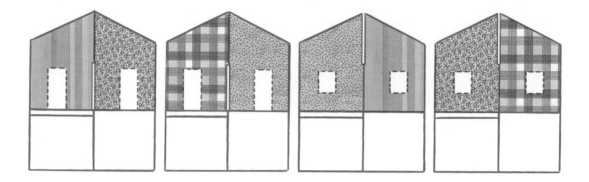

2 Draw a vertical line up the center of each piece of chipboard. Mark the center of each vertical line. These two pieces will be notched together. On one piece measure up from the bottom 7" (18cm). Mark with pencil. On the other piece measure down from the top 7" (18cm). Following these lines, cut out a narrow strip of chipboard roughly the width of the thickness of the chipboard.

3 Try out the notches. Deepen as necessary.

4 Cut four 10" x 10" (25.5cm x 25.5cm) pieces of thin birch plywood. Attach floor pieces to house pieces following the diagram. Make sure you apply the tape to the underside of the floor.

5 Once the floor pieces are attached, set up your house. Once assembled, determine which wallpapers you want for which rooms. Mark the names of these colors or patterns with pencil on both walls of each room. This will help you remember which wallpaper to adhere where once your house has been disassembled.

6 Cut out the wallpaper: Cut out eight pieces of four different paper types that measure 14" x 10" (35.5cm x 25.5cm). Pair up the four different paper styles. Determine the left and right side pieces and cut the roof peak, measuring down 4" (10cm) to create the angle.

7 Disassemble the house. Lay one house piece flat on a piece of scrap cardboard. Cover the floor pieces with additional scrap cardboard to block them from the mounting spray. Apply mounting spray over the wall section of the house and apply the wallpaper

pieces according to your notes. Set aside and allow to dry. Repeat with the other house piece. Trim off any excess paper that extends beyond the chipboard. Flip them over and repeat the process on the other sides.

8 Cutting doors and windows: Cut the windows in one piece of the house, and cut doors in the other piece so that when they interlock, each room will have one door and one window.

9 Create a window template by cutting out scrap paper or board that measures 3½" x 3" (9cm x 7.5cm).

10 Take the piece of the house you've chosen for the windows. Measure 2½" (6.5cm) in from the outer edge of the house, and 3" (7.5cm) up from the floor of the house. Place the corner of your window template here. Trace your template with a pencil and then cut along these lines with a utility knife. Use a ruler or a straightedge to guide your blade. Repeat for the other side of the house piece.

11. Create a door template by cutting out a piece of scrap paper or board that measures 6½" x 3" (16.5cm x 7.5cm).

12. Take the second piece of the house and measure 2½" (6.5cm) in from the side to mark where the door will be. Place the template at this point, trace it, and cut it out with a utility knife. Repeat for the other side of the house piece.

You can also freehand the doors and windows or cut out your own shapes. Just make sure that neither doors nor windows are too close to the edges of the house, as this will compromise the strength of the walls.

13. Are you ready to move in?

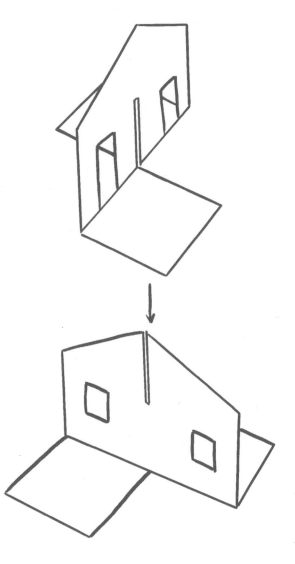

YOU GOT MAIL — family mailbox

FINISHED MEASUREMENTS: 7" X 7" X 11" (18CM X 18CM X 28CM)

Snail mail is unfortunately getting lost in our fast paced, e-mail culture. Our little ones, however, seem to appreciate the excitement of the handwritten word, the thoughtful note, the anticipation of opening an envelope. With this simple project, help nurture and cherish this beautiful tradition and save it from extinction.

MATERIALS

- ▶ **Family Mailbox template (page 155)**
- ▶ **single-ply grayboard**
- ▶ **2"- (5cm-) wide gummed paper tape**
- ▶ **recycled envelopes, to use interior patterns**
- ▶ **decoupage glue**
- ▶ **one tongue depressor**
- ▶ **red acrylic paint**
- ▶ **red felt**
- ▶ **Clear Gel tacky glue**
- ▶ **two brass fasteners**
- ▶ **thin elastic**
- ▶ **one medium-sized bead**

TOOLS

- ▶ **craft knife**
- ▶ **cutting mat**
- ▶ **scissors**
- ▶ **small 1" (2.5cm) flat paintbrush**
- ▶ **ruler**
- ▶ **drill with bits**

instructions

1. Using a craft knife, cut a rectangle of grayboard that is 11" x 17" (28cm x 43cm). This will be the "roof" of your mailbox. Grayboard has grain so it is easier to bend in one direction, rather than the other. Before cutting, gently bow the board to see in which direction it bends more easily and make that the longer (17"/43cm) side.

2. Cut another piece of grayboard that is 7" x 11" (18cm x 28cm). This will be the base of your

mailbox. The direction you cut this board doesn't matter, as it won't be bent.

3 Lay the pieces of board next to each other with their 11" (28cm) sides just slightly apart. To use gummed tape: Flip the tape shiny side up, and brush with water. The shiny side is now an active adhesive. Lay a piece of gummed paper over the seam to connect these two pieces. Allow to dry.

4 Once dry, gently bend the "roof" piece, forming a U shape, and attach it to the other side of the base with another piece of gummed tape. Allow to dry.

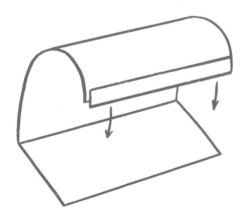

5 Flip the mailbox on its end and trace this U shape onto another piece of board. Repeat.

6 Cut these two shapes out. They will serve as the back of the mailbox and its front door.

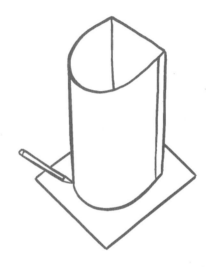

7 To attach the back piece: Start by attaching the bottom of the back piece first (the flat side) with a 7"- (18cm-) long piece of gummed tape, and continue to attach the rounded edges with smaller pieces of gummed tape. Allow to dry.

8 In the meantime, cut out medium-sized pieces of paper from your envelopes. Adhere them to the mailbox using decoupage glue. A patchwork approach, mixing and matching patterns, works nicely.

9 Cover the unattached door piece with decorative papers. For the rounded door and the back pieces, feel free to adhere papers that extend beyond the edges of the piece. These parts can be trimmed off later. Allow to dry. Trim off excess paper. Coat the entire exterior of the mailbox with decoupage glue as a final protective layer and allow to dry.

10 Lay the door piece with the decorated side down at the mouth of the mailbox, set just slightly apart from it. Apply a strip of gummed tape across the seam, in the interior of the mailbox so it won't be visible when the mailbox is closed.

11 To make the flag, paint the tongue depressor red with the acrylic paint. Set aside to dry.

12 Cut a piece of red felt using the mailbox flag template. Cut the mailbox heart out of paper. Adhere the heart to the felt using tacky glue.

13 Drill a hole at one end of the depressor large enough to push the arms of a brass fastener through. On the right side of the mailbox measure 2½" (6.5cm) up from the base and 1½" (3.8cm) back from the door. This will mark where you are attaching the flag. Make a small mark and drill a hole. Use a brass fastener to attach the flag to this point.

14. To make the latch, at the peak of the box, measure ¾" (2cm) back from the mouth of the mailbox. Drill a small hole. Thread your bead with the elastic and put the ends of the thread down through the hole. Knot securely and trim loose ends.

15. On the door of the mailbox, measure ¾" (2cm) down from the top at its peak. Drill a small hole large enough to stick the arms of a brass fastener through. Make a loop of elastic that is large enough to reach from this point to the bead now affixed to the top of the mailbox. Thread ends of the loop through the hole at the top of the door. Place the brass fastener in this hole. Knot the loop over the arms of the brass fastener

16. Let the fan mail pour in!

▶ KID FUN

MAKE YOUR OWN ENVELOPES

On page 155 you will find a template to make mini-envelopes out of any paper! Enlarge it 200 percent, then choose your favorite paper, cut, and fold! We used shaped scissors with a decorative edge to convert any found image into stamps.

You could use the Letters templates on page 128 to write your family name on the mailbox, for instance "the Smiths."

PEEKABOO HOUSE

cardboard playhouse

LEVEL: ☐   **FINISHED MEASUREMENTS:** 36" X 24" X 24" (91CM X 61CM X 61CM)

MATERIALS

▶ **Cardboard Playhouse templates (pages 156-57)**

▶ **24" x 24" x 24" (61cm x 61cm x 61cm) cardboard box**

▶ **various papers**

▶ **various tapes**

▶ **large piece of wallpaper**

TOOLS

▶ **craft knife**

▶ **scissors**

▶ **ruler**

Half playhouse, half photo-op, this project gives a new life to a plain shipping box. This fun and fast project becomes the little hideaway or the home away from home that most toddlers need at one point or another.

instructions

1   Place the box on the floor. Determine which side will be the top and which will be the bottom. Cut off the four bottom flaps. Set flaps aside.

2   For the door: On the front of the house measure 6" (15cm) from the top and 6" (15cm) from each side. Draw a rectangle with a pencil. Cut the top horizontal part of this rectangle and the right vertical side, leaving the left vertical side uncut. For this side make a light cut to score the hinge of the door. Two inches from the top of the door center the door window template. Trace this shape and cut it out.

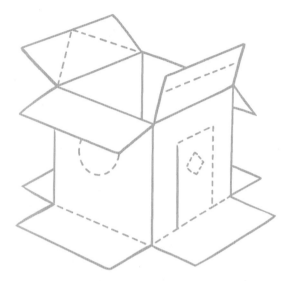

that will support the winged roof. For the front flap, cut it down so that it is 6" (15cm) in height. Fold this piece inside the house for added wall strength.

5 Now take two of the flaps that you cut from the bottom of the house and tape them onto your roof sides so that they overlap and meet, resting on the triangle at the back. Make sure to tape from the inside and the outside.

3 For the peekaboo: Place the lion face template 9¼" (23.5cm) in from each side and 5" (12.5cm) from the top of the box. Cut out.

4 Two of the top flaps will meet to form the roof. For the other two sides, the back will stand upright to support the roof at the back of the house, and the front will be trimmed and folded inward to provide stability at the front of the house. Determine which flap will be the back of the house. With the back flap extended, mark the middle at 12" (30.5cm). Trace a line from each of the two bottom corners where the flap starts to the middle, forming a triangle. Now cut with a craft knife following these lines so that you have a triangle

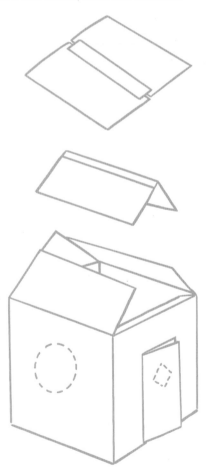

PETIT COLLAGE

6. Cut a rectangle of wallpaper that is 17" x 15" (43cm x 38cm). This will be your lion body. On the bottom of the rectangle measure a 6" x 8" (15cm x 20.5cm) piece, centering it lengthwise so the front and back legs of the lion are each 4½" (11cm) wide.

   As you're cutting, round the top two corners of this cutout and also the upper right corner of the lion body.

7. On the side of the house with the cut out circle, adhere the lion body, aligning the left side of the lion body with the center of the cut out circle, and positioning it so that the legs are nearly touching the base of the house.

8. Using the template, cut 6 lion mane pieces out of decorative paper. Adhere the paper pieces around the edge of the cut out circle to form a mane. Finish off the house with fun tape and sticker details.

9. Peekaboo smile!

tips

▶ You can adapt this project to any oversize box you find. Just make sure your child fits in it sitting down and there is an opening or door big enough for him to easily get in and out.

▶ You can customize the peekaboo animal or even make a different one on the other side.

BASIC TECHNIQUES

Although cutting and pasting seems fairly basic, there are few tricks of the trade.

CUTTING

Precise cutting is half the battle with a lot of these projects. Of course, each paper presents its own unique challenges, but choosing the right tools is essential to this type of crafting. Each project in the book notes whether you require a pair of scissors or a craft knife.

- ▶ When you are using scissors keep in mind that the paper should be moving, feeding into the scissors—not the other way around.

- ▶ When you are using a craft knife for straight cuts, choose a good metal ruler, and remember to replace the blade often.

CRAFTING WITH DECOUPAGE

Decoupage is a complicated word for an easy technique that requires simple materials: paper, scissors, glue, and a brush. Decoupage is commonly associated with Victorian flowers or silhouettes of classic nature images applied to furniture, but here I use it in a fresh and modern way.

You can decoupage just about anything, but this book focuses mostly on adhering paper onto cardboard, wood, and tin.

Although cutting and pasting seems fairly basic, there are a few tricks of the trade.

- ▶ Be mindful of the paper your image is on. Papers that are too thin may wrinkle. Some colored papers may "bleed" when coated with glue, so test out a corner or a scrap of the paper first if you are uncertain.

- ▶ Our decoupage glue of choice is Mod Podge, a popular water-based two-in-one adhesive and sealant. We find it to be very strong without being watery or gummy. When choosing your adhesive, be sure to check the label to see if it's recommended for paper. Another popular option for decoupage glue is an acrylic matte medium.

1. Start by brushing an even coat of decoupage glue onto your chosen surface. It is important that the entire surface is coated and that there are no lumps of adhesive. This will ensure that the paper sticks completely to the surface and that there are no bubbles.

2. Lay down the paper you are adhering, then brush a second coat of decoupage

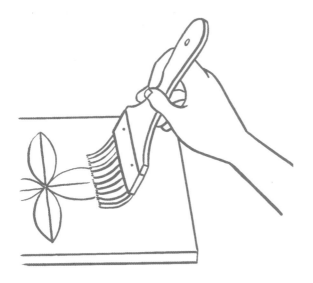

glue over the top of the paper. Brushing over the top of the paper will help push the paper down securely, as well as seal its surface with a protective coating.

If you see air bubbles trapped under the paper, try pricking it lightly with a pushpin to release the air, then carefully smooth out the paper with your fingers.

3. Allow to dry. You can add another protective coat over the entire piece. Allow to dry again.

If extra protection is needed, especially for an item that will be heavily used, such as the play table (page 59) or step stool (page 75), add a coat of polyurethane varnish to protect the piece.

4. As with many things, practice makes perfect.

WORKING WITH WOOD AND METAL

The Petit Collage line uses a lot of natural materials, such as wood or wood veneer. You can source wood readily at home improvement stores or you can use pieces that you already have.

New, unfinished wood requires little pretreating. Depending on the type of piece or lumber, it may need some light sanding, and you are good to go. However, since this book encourages recycling and upcycling, you may find pieces of wood that have already been treated or finished.

If the piece is painted and in good condition, you may choose to leave as is and adhere papers onto it. If the paint is distressed, you will need to strip away the paint with the chemical remover appropriate to that paint type. There are several options: some liquid, some gel, some in spray form. Seek advice at your local hardware store on the right solution.

If the piece is waxed or oiled, you may need to treat the surface with mineral spirits so that the water-based glue doesn't react to it and provoke peeling (the last thing we want).

If you are buying a vintage piece of furniture, make sure it is free of bugs (no holes) and that the construction is sturdy.

Tin and metal are easier materials to work with, as long as you make sure there is no rust.

RESOURCES

Found papers, the main material for this book, can be sourced anywhere—from your very own mailbox to flea markets, estate and garage sales, and used library book sales.

Most of the supplies listed below can be found at your local arts and crafts shop, home improvement store, or office supply store. I have listed some online resources for items that may not be as easily available, but check your local store first. And of course, check your local thrift stores, too. When you can, repurpose and upcycle. You may even have some things at home just waiting to be used.

GENERAL ART AND CRAFT SUPPLIES
Dick Blick
www.dickblick.com

Michaels
www.michaels.com

HARDWARE AND LUMBER
Home Depot
www.homedepot.com

ONLINE VINTAGE RESOURCES
Etsy
www.etsy.com

eBay
www.ebay.com

SOURCES FOR SPECIFIC MATERIALS
Personalized Baby Plaque (page 33)
The wood panel is available at Dick Blick (www.dickblick.com).

Most art stores sell wood cradle boards. For a variety of sizes, check www.walnuthollow.com.

Baby Door Tag (page 37)
Find cotton ribbon at your local sewing supply store. Four-inch (10cm) cork coasters will be available at a craft supply store.

Bird Growth Chart (page 39)
Number stickers can be found in an art supply store.

Patterned Letters (page 45)
Source vintage letters if possible or purchase new letters from a craft store, such as Michaels (www.michaels.com).

Cityscape Wood Veneer Headboard (page 47)
A large selection of washi tape is available at Wishy Washi Tape (www.wishywashi.com).

Wood veneer with adhesive backing is available at Wood-All (www.wood-all.com).

Wheeled Toy Bin (page 51)
Source a vintage crate at a flea market or vintage shop. Find casters at a home improvement store.

Bunny Wall Clock (page 55)
The embroidery hoop and felt can be found at any craft or sewing supply store. Find wood veneer at an art or craft supply store.

Play Table (page 59)
Plywood can be purchased and cut to size at your local home improvement store. Wood legs are available at Home Depot (www.homedepot.com).

Book Ledges (page 61)
Find 2x2s at your local home improvement store.

The basswood pieces can be found at an art supply store.

Family Memo Board (page 67)
Chalkboard contact paper is available at Con-Tact (www.contactbrand.com).

Cork trivets can be found at home improvement stores, kitchen supply stores, or Ikea (www.ikea.com).

Dry-Erase Dinner Planner (page 69)
Buy a frame from an art store, frame shop, or source a frame from your local thrift shop.

Window Film Cutouts (page 73)
Etched glass film is available at Artscape (www.artscape-inc.com).

Step Stool (page 75)
Apple boxes are available at most photo supply stores. Find them online at Calumet (www.calumetphoto.com).

Memory Box (page 79)
A variety of wood boxes are available at Walnut Hollow (www.walnuthollow.com).

Family Gallery (page 81)
Homasote is available at most lumber or builders supply stores. Bulldog clips and oversized rubber bands are available at art supply stores.

Friends Coat Rack (page 85)
Plywood can be purchased and cut to size at your local home improvement store. If possible, try to salvage scraps from other home improvement projects. Find knobs at a home improvement store or a building salvage store.

Ceiling Pendant (page 89)
Cord kits are available from most home improvement stores and some home decor stores. Chipboard is available at art supply stores.

Custom Baby Blocks (page 95)
Plain wood blocks can be purchased at Woodworks Ltd. (www.craftparts.com).

Toy Drum (page 101)
Wood dowels and balls are available at most craft stores.

Memory Game (page 105)
Repurpose a found tin or purchase a new container from a home organization store such as The Container Store (www.containerstore.com).

TEMPLATES

ABCDEFGHIJ

KLMNOPQRS

TUVWXYZ

numbers

1 2 3 4 5
6 7 8 9 0

paper mobile

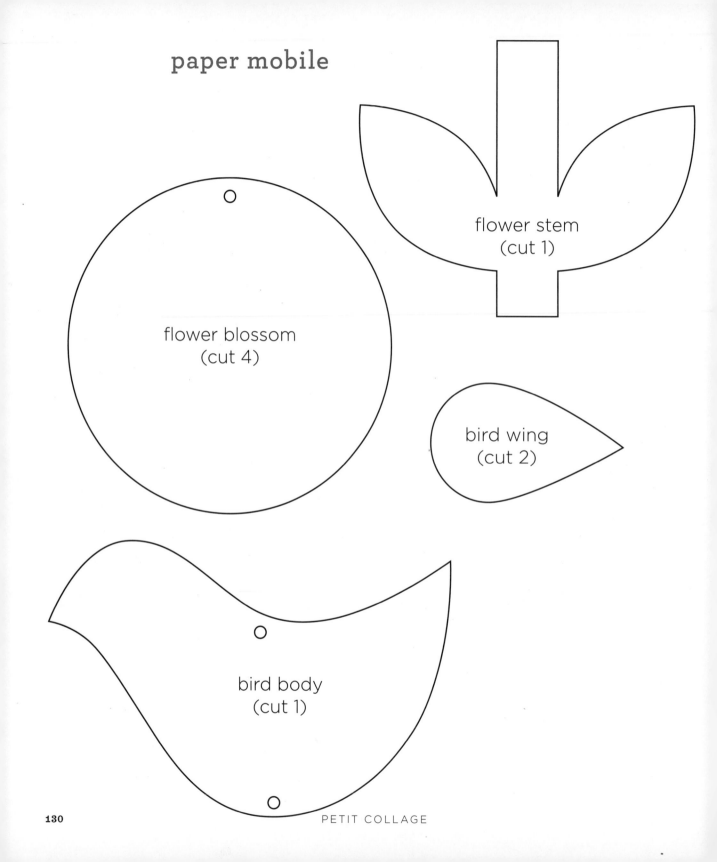

flower stem
(cut 1)

flower blossom
(cut 4)

bird wing
(cut 2)

bird body
(cut 1)

PETIT COLLAGE

personalized baby plaque

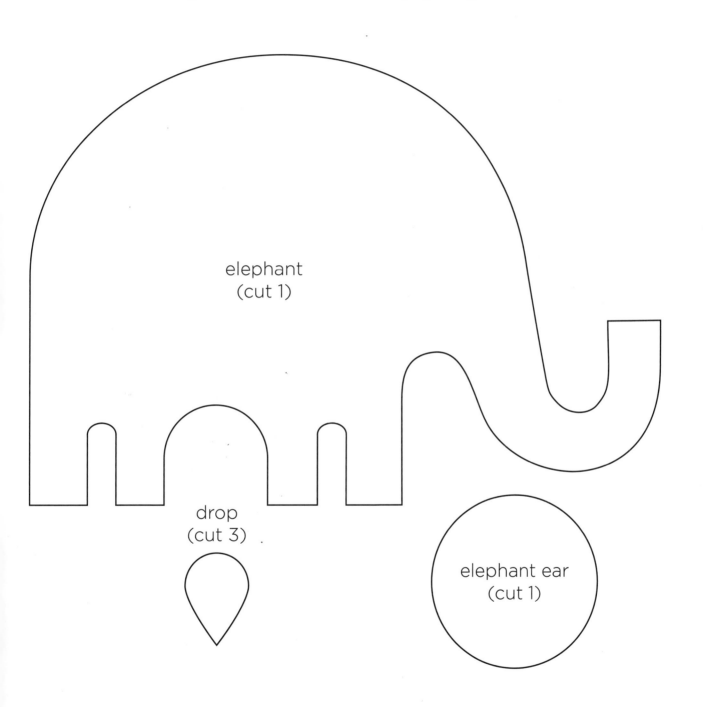

elephant
(cut 1)

drop
(cut 3)

elephant ear
(cut 1)

baby door tag

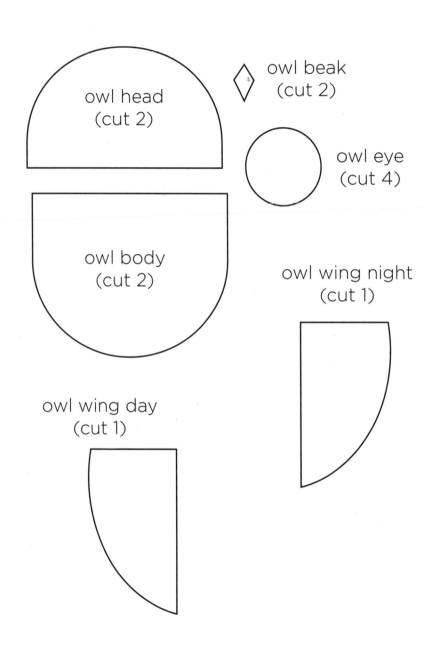

owl head
(cut 2)

owl beak
(cut 2)

owl eye
(cut 4)

owl body
(cut 2)

owl wing night
(cut 1)

owl wing day
(cut 1)

bird growth chart

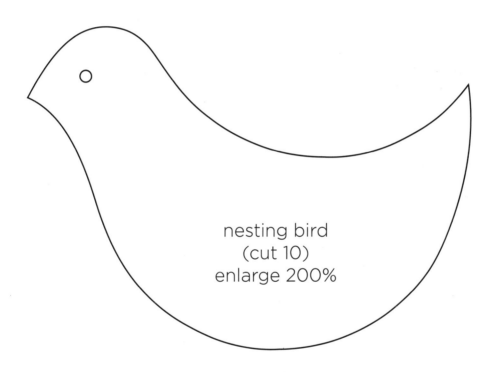

nesting bird
(cut 10)
enlarge 200%

cityscape wood veneer headboard

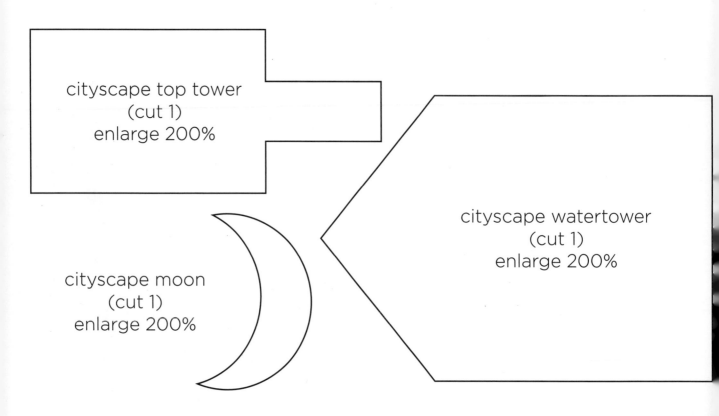

cityscape top tower
(cut 1)
enlarge 200%

cityscape moon
(cut 1)
enlarge 200%

cityscape watertower
(cut 1)
enlarge 200%

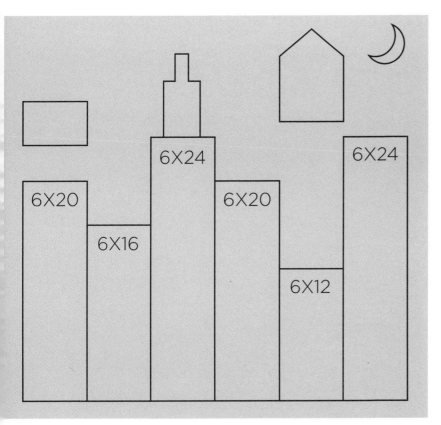

wood veneer headboard guide

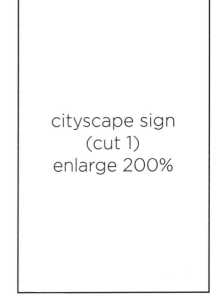

cityscape sign
(cut 1)
enlarge 200%

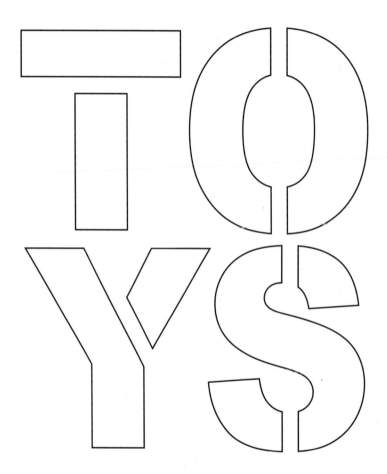

toy bin text
(cut 1)
enlarge 200%

wall clock

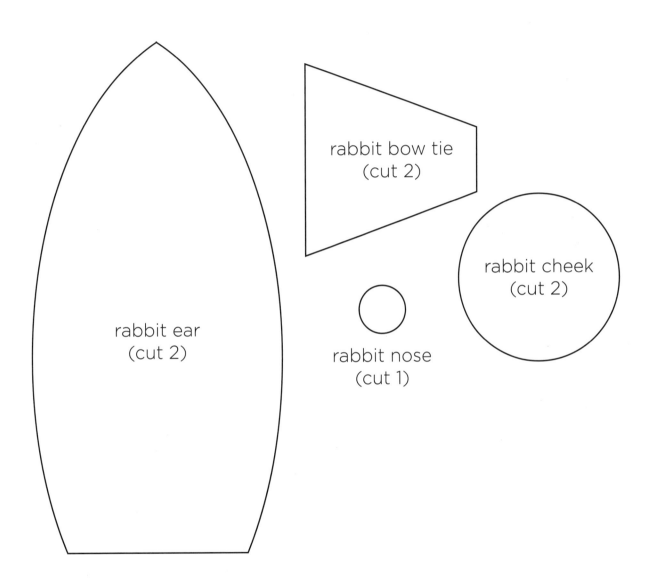

rabbit ear
(cut 2)

rabbit bow tie
(cut 2)

rabbit cheek
(cut 2)

rabbit nose
(cut 1)

window film cutouts

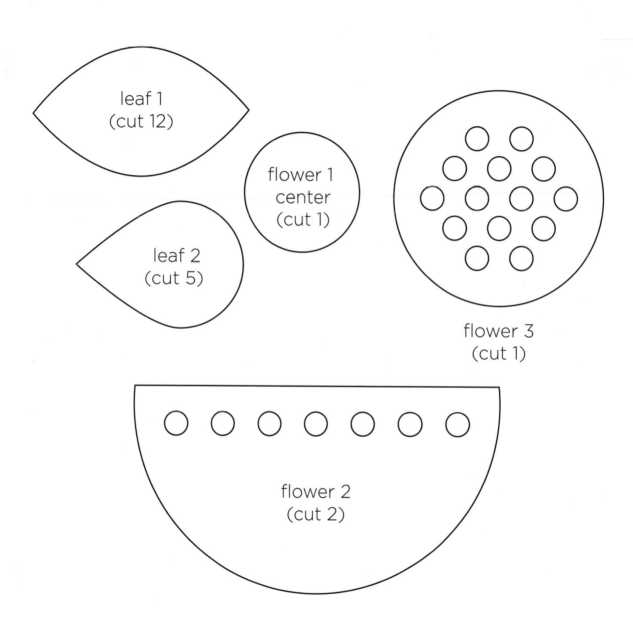

leaf 1
(cut 12)

flower 1
center
(cut 1)

leaf 2
(cut 5)

flower 3
(cut 1)

flower 2
(cut 2)

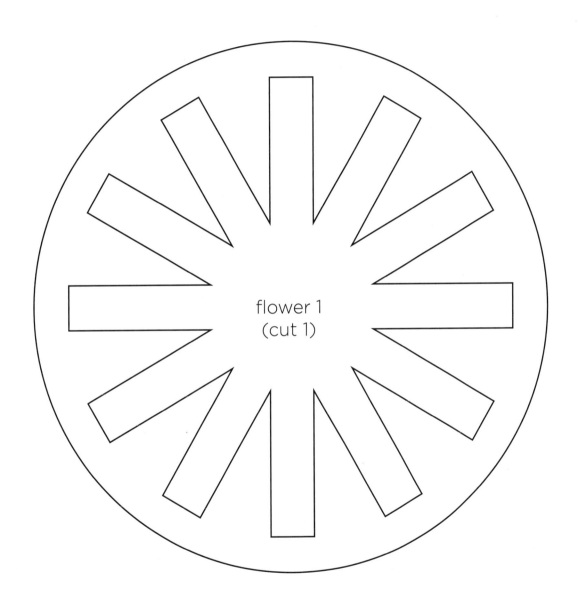

flower 1
(cut 1)

step stool

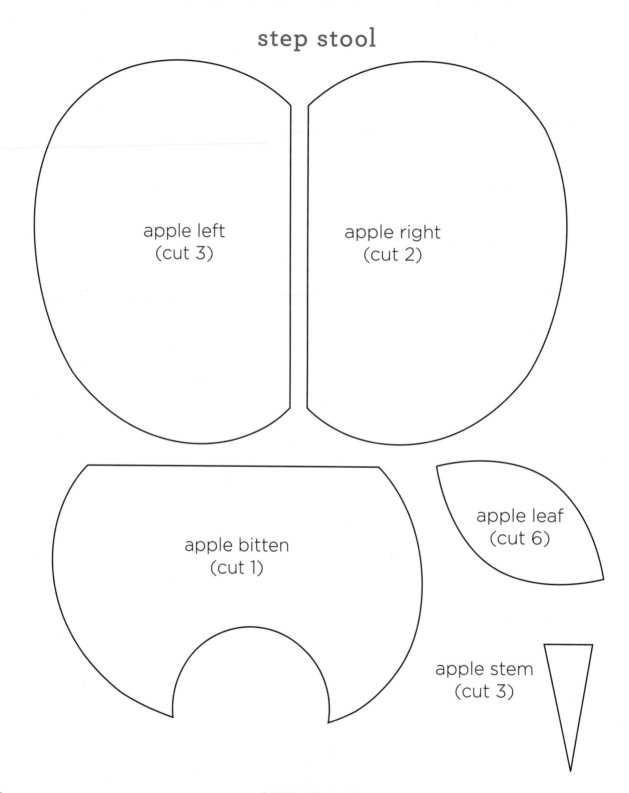

apple left
(cut 3)

apple right
(cut 2)

apple bitten
(cut 1)

apple leaf
(cut 6)

apple stem
(cut 3)

memory box

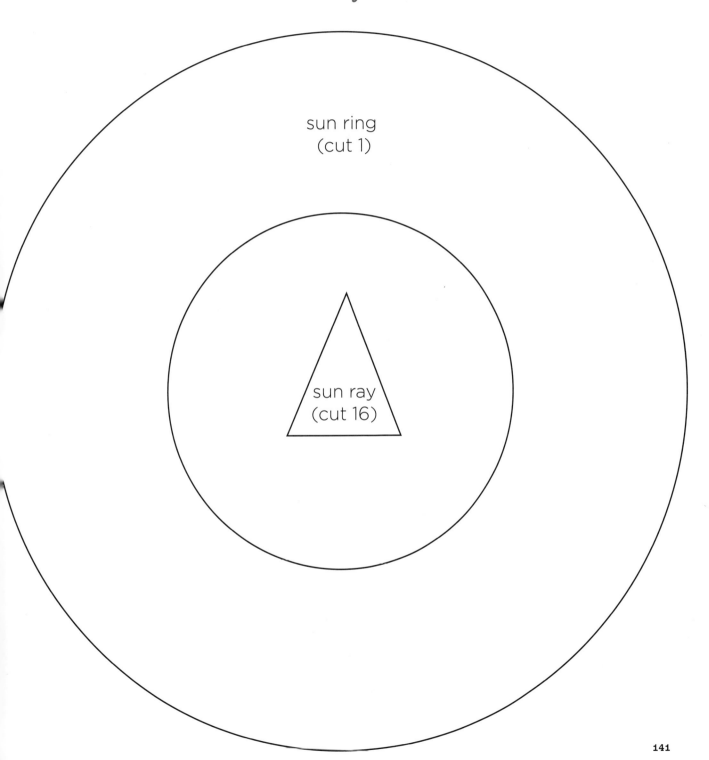

sun ring
(cut 1)

sun ray
(cut 16)

friends coat rack

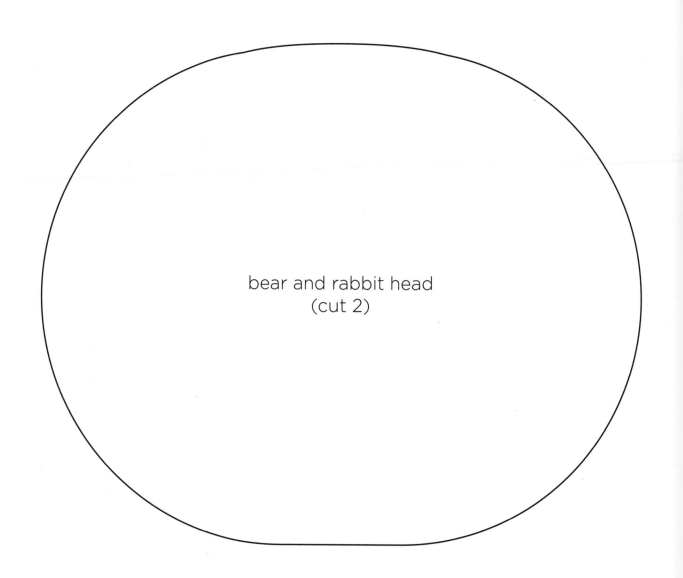

bear and rabbit head
(cut 2)

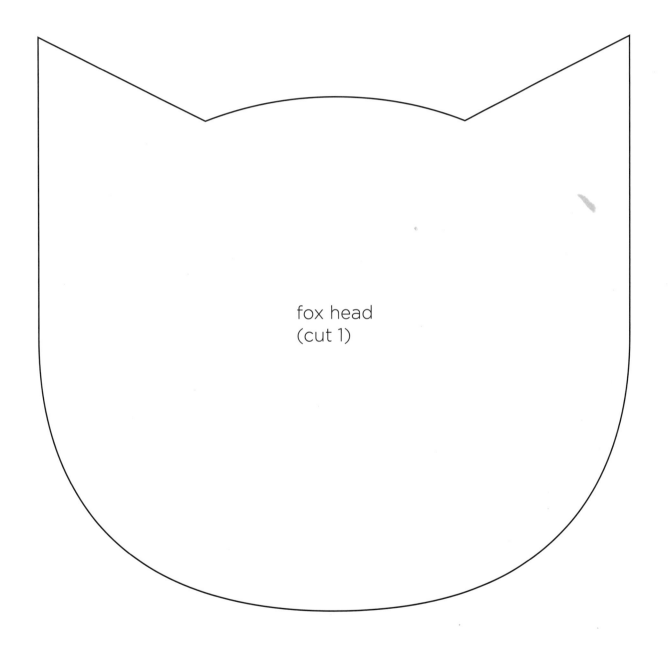

fox head
(cut 1)

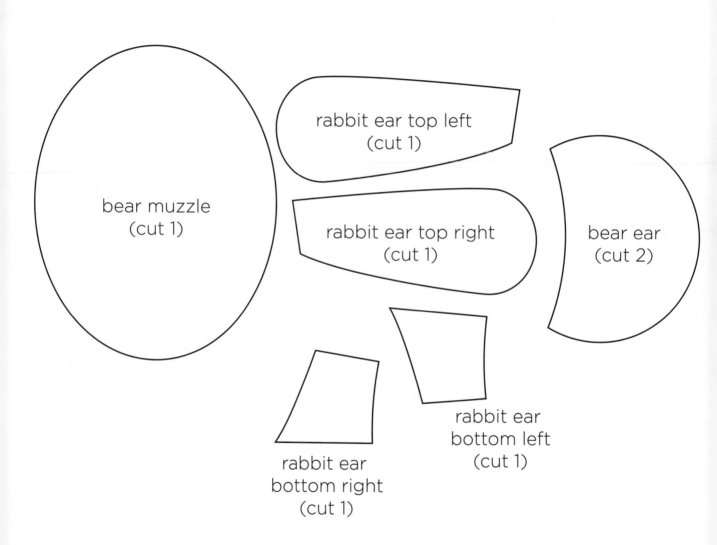

bear muzzle
(cut 1)

rabbit ear top left
(cut 1)

rabbit ear top right
(cut 1)

bear ear
(cut 2)

rabbit ear
bottom left
(cut 1)

rabbit ear
bottom right
(cut 1)

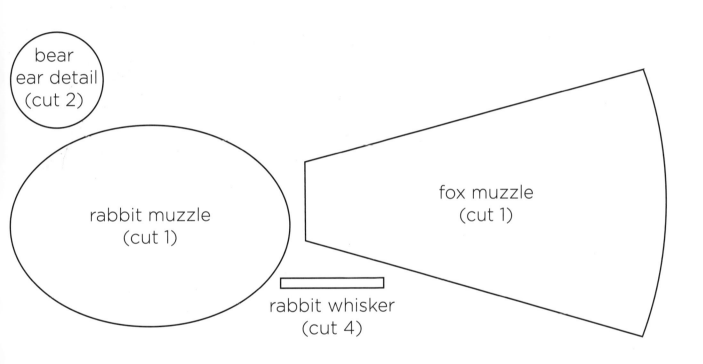

bear
ear detail
(cut 2)

rabbit muzzle
(cut 1)

fox muzzle
(cut 1)

rabbit whisker
(cut 4)

ceiling pendant

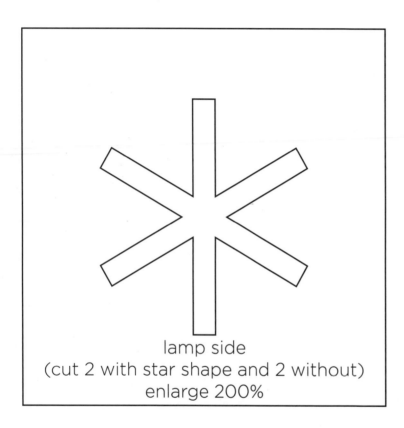

lamp side
(cut 2 with star shape and 2 without)
enlarge 200%

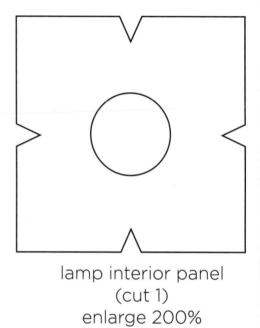

lamp interior panel
(cut 1)
enlarge 200%

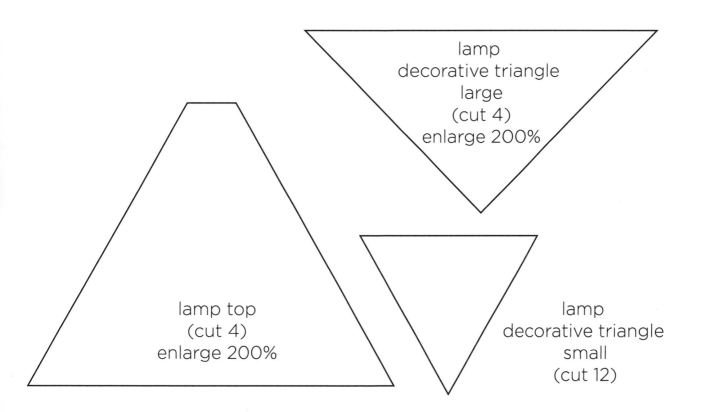

lamp
decorative triangle
large
(cut 4)
enlarge 200%

lamp top
(cut 4)
enlarge 200%

lamp
decorative triangle
small
(cut 12)

custom baby blocks

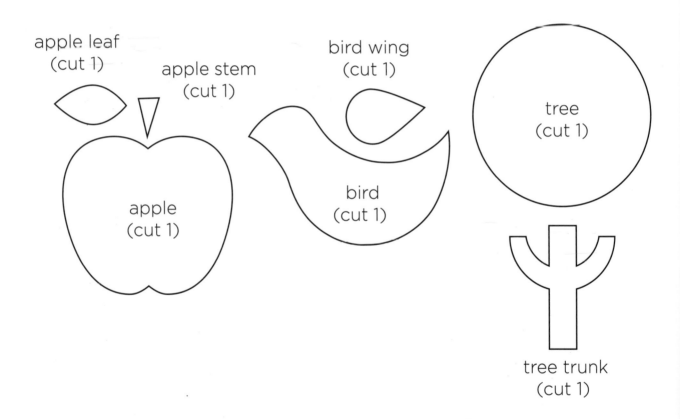

apple leaf
(cut 1)

apple stem
(cut 1)

apple
(cut 1)

bird wing
(cut 1)

bird
(cut 1)

tree
(cut 1)

tree trunk
(cut 1)

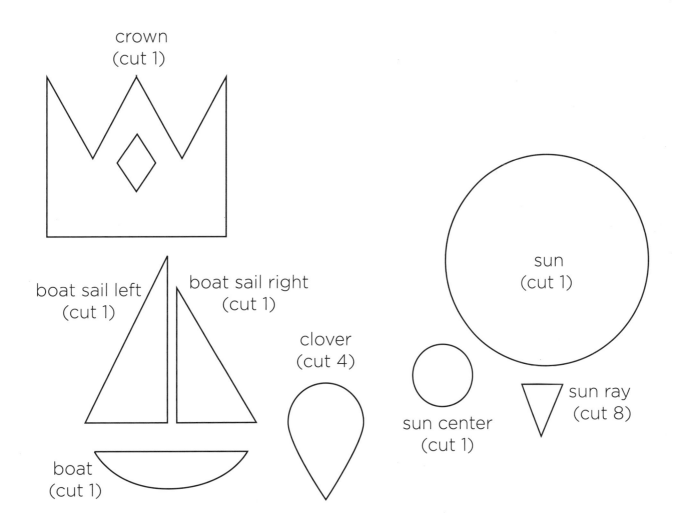

crown
(cut 1)

boat sail left
(cut 1)

boat sail right
(cut 1)

clover
(cut 4)

sun
(cut 1)

sun center
(cut 1)

sun ray
(cut 8)

boat
(cut 1)

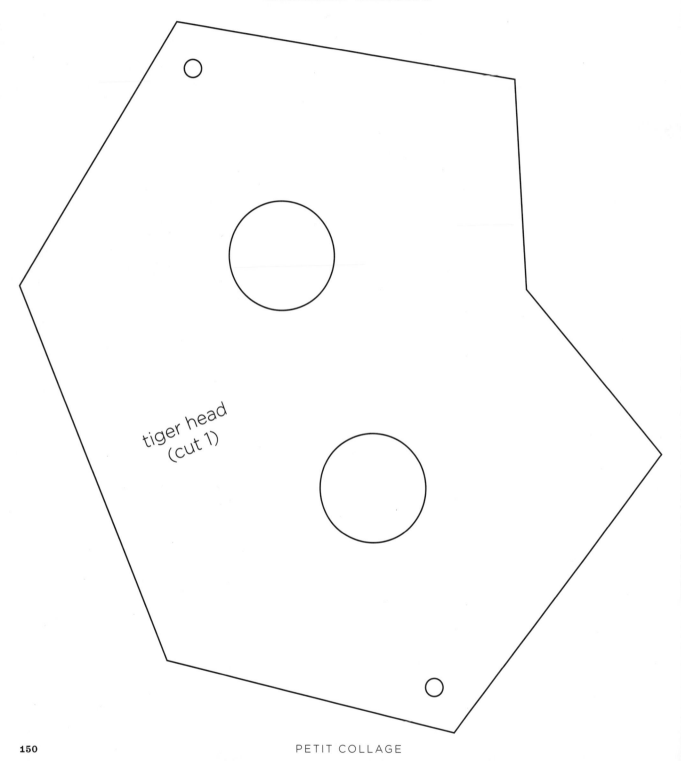

tiger head
(cut 1)

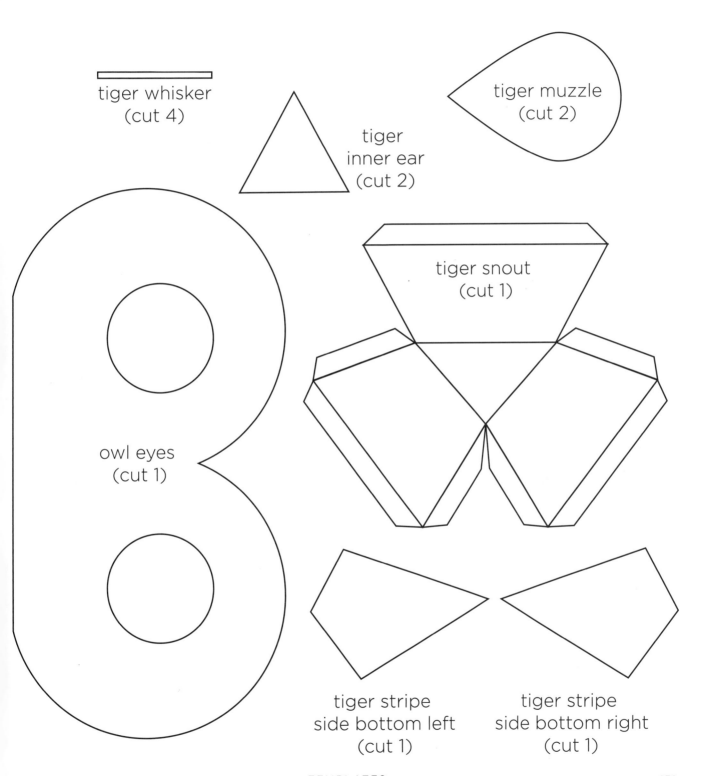

tiger whisker
(cut 4)

tiger muzzle
(cut 2)

tiger
inner ear
(cut 2)

tiger snout
(cut 1)

owl eyes
(cut 1)

tiger stripe
side bottom left
(cut 1)

tiger stripe
side bottom right
(cut 1)

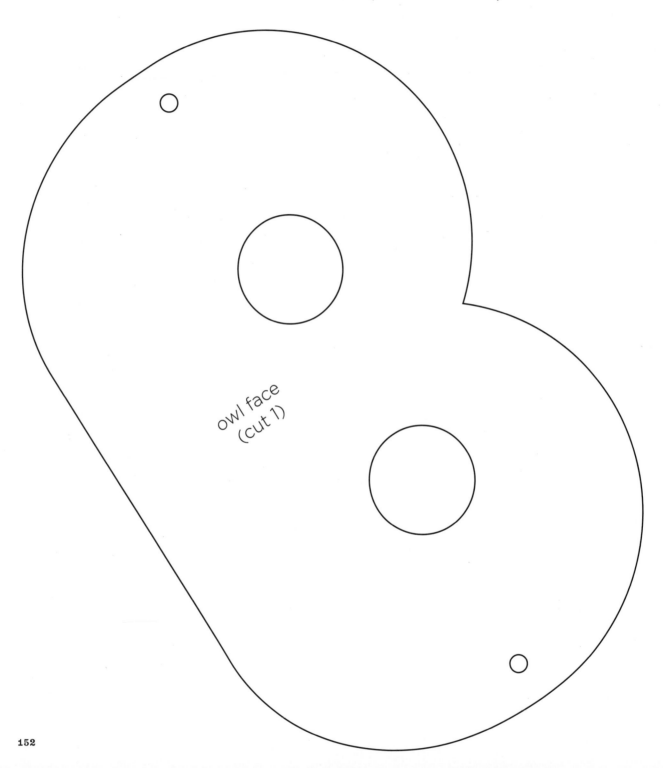

owl face
(cut 1)

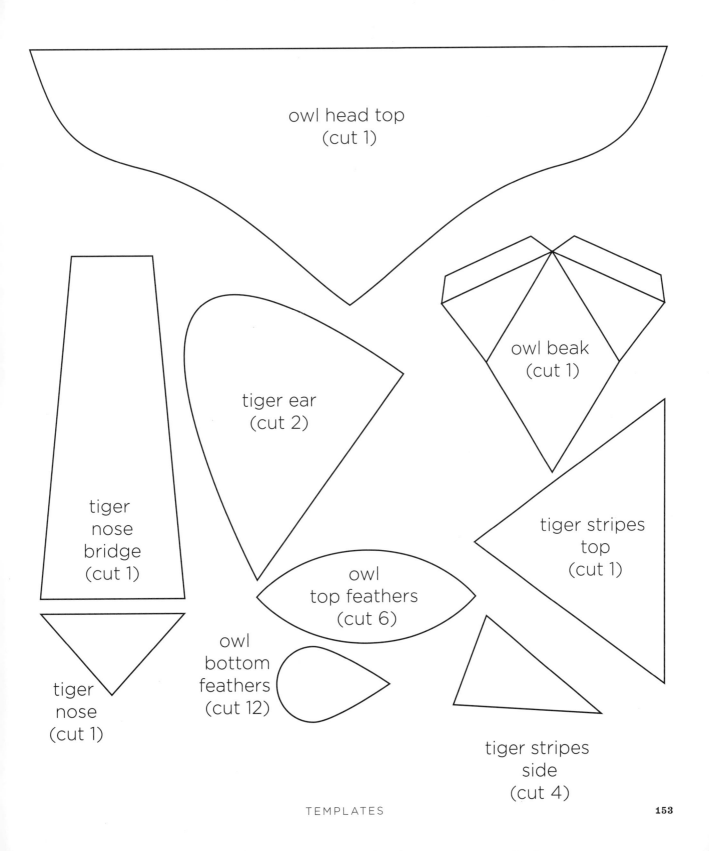

owl head top
(cut 1)

owl beak
(cut 1)

tiger ear
(cut 2)

tiger
nose
bridge
(cut 1)

tiger stripes
top
(cut 1)

owl
top feathers
(cut 6)

owl
bottom
feathers
(cut 12)

tiger
nose
(cut 1)

tiger stripes
side
(cut 4)

toy drum

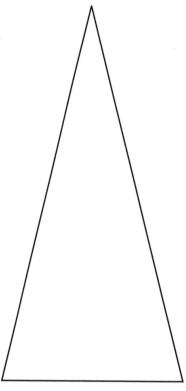

drum triangle
(cut 12 to16 pieces)

family mailbox

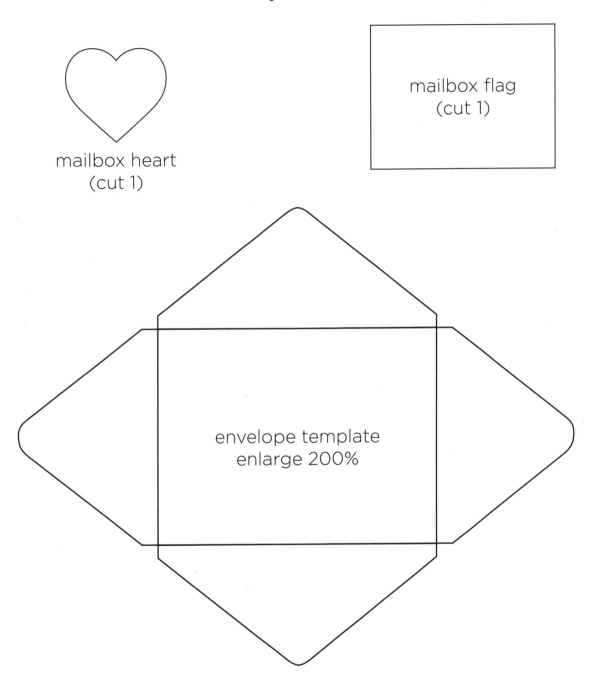

mailbox flag
(cut 1)

mailbox heart
(cut 1)

envelope template
enlarge 200%

cardboard playhouse

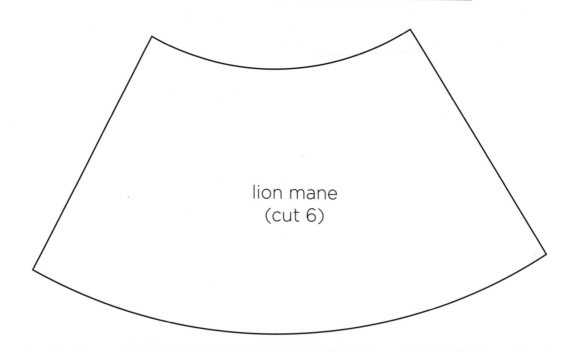

door window
(cut out 1)

lion mane
(cut 6)

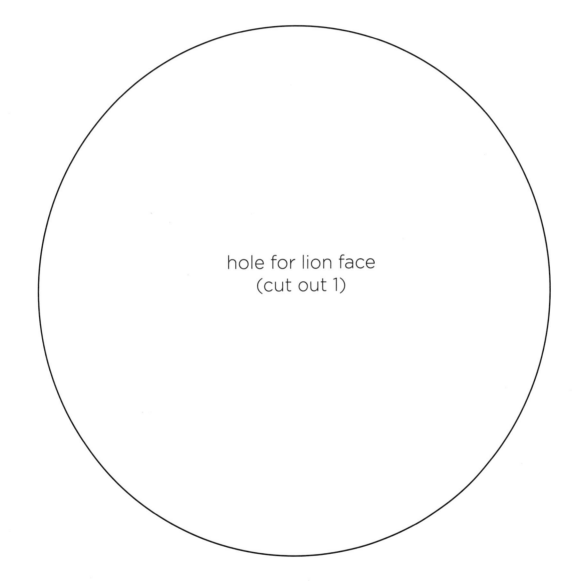

hole for lion face
(cut out 1)

ABOUT THE AUTHOR

Lorena Siminovich is a designer, children's book author and illustrator, entrepreneur, and multitasker extraordinaire. She has published more than twenty children's books in more than ten countries and is the founder of Petit Collage.

What started with a handmade collage for a friend's baby shower is now a modern lifestyle brand of décor and playthings for young families, found in stores the world over. A mom herself, Lorena is passionate about creating sustainably made and visually appealing items for the entire family.

Growing up in Buenos Aires, she was surrounded by art, mid-century graphics, and a lush Latin American color palette which greatly influenced her work. After a few years in New York, she now calls San Francisco her home and lives in a mid-century house on a hill with her husband and daughter.

ABOUT PETIT COLLAGE

Started in 2006, Petit Collage is all about well-designed goods for modern families. From wall décor and mobiles to toys and dolls, playfulness imbues every product.

Lead by Lorena Siminovich, the studio, located in an artistic hub of San Francisco, is an incubator of new ideas, art, and illustration where creating great design and pushing the envelope with new formats is the norm. Striving to handcraft their goods in a sustainable way, using the best-quality, most forest-friendly materials available, is equally important. Sure to delight and inspire children and grown-ups alike and found in homes the world over, these goods are perfect for the nursery yet sophisticated enough for any room in the contemporary home.

Petit Collage is well loved by the media and has been featured on *The Martha Stewart Show,* the *New York Times, The Wall Street Journal, Dwell* magazine, and leading blogs such as *Design*Sponge, Decor8,* and *Design Mom,* among others.

INDEX